# GROWING TOGETHER

## Developing and Sustaining a Community of Practice in Early Childhood

Kathi Gillaspy, MEd
Megan Vinh, PhD
Nancy Surbrook-Goins
Sarah Nichols



Gryphon House
www.gryphonhouse.com

Published by Gryphon House, Inc.
P. O. Box 10, Lewisville, NC 27023
800.638.0928; 877.638.7576 (fax)
Visit us on the web at www.gryphonhouse.com.



Library of Congress Control Number:2019943628

**Bulk Purchase**
Gryphon House books are available for special premiums and sales promotions as well as for fund-raising use. Special editions or book excerpts also can be created to specifications. For details, call 800.638.0928.

**Disclaimer**
Gryphon House, Inc., cannot be held responsible for damage, mishap, or injury incurred during the use of or because of activities in this book. Appropriate and reasonable caution and adult supervision of children involved in activities and corresponding to the age and capability of each child involved are recommended at all times. Do not leave children unattended at any time. Observe safety and caution at all times.

# TABLE OF CONTENTS

# INTRODUCTION

## Who Should Use This Book?

We hope this book will be used by our partners in the field of early childhood, such as early interventionists, special educators, administrators, professional-development consultants, technical-assistance providers, program directors, teachers, child-care providers, students and professors of early childhood development and education, service coordinators, and home visitors. This book can be used by one person to explore or reflect individually, or it can be used by programs or teams to establish a community of practice (CoP). It can support preservice and in-service coursework to help prepare new early childhood professionals, to support practicing professionals in their daily work, and to assist state agencies in furthering professional learning in their locations. Most importantly, it can help individuals determine how a CoP can further their own learning and can provide them with the tools to begin one.

## The Purpose of This Book

This book explains what a CoP is and how you can start one. Regardless of your job title or where you are in your professional career, you can create your own CoP with others who share your interests. This book discusses how to successfully begin, sustain, and facilitate a CoP and how to collect data on a CoP's effectiveness to support growth and change within the CoP over time.

## How This Book Is Organized

We, the authors, have developed and sustained multiple kinds of communities of practice (CoPs) in various early childhood settings, and we are excited to share what we believe works in the field. This book includes the following steps for developing, cultivating, and sustaining a CoP:

- Finding a shared interest, shared practice, or both to explore
- Promoting your CoP and inviting people to join
- Creating the structure for your CoP
- Building a sense of fellowship among members
- Promoting member engagement and investment within and outside of meetings*
- Facilitating effectively
- Evaluating a CoP
- Collecting and using ongoing data about a CoP

A study guide appears at the end of each chapter to help you consider your own experiences related to CoPs and how CoPs can enhance your professional development. More importantly, the questions will help you explore what you need from a CoP and how you might form one. As you answer the questions, you can also note your own queries and thoughts and capture your ideas about how to start, develop, and sustain your own CoP. Ideally, you will watch your understanding evolve as you go through this book.

*In this book, unless otherwise specified, the term *meeting* refers to any CoP gathering, whether in person or virtual (such as conference calls or video chats)

CHAPTER 1

# DEFINING A COMMUNITY OF PRACTICE

## What Is a Community of Practice?

CoPs, both formal and informal, are everywhere. Whether you realize it or not, you have probably been part of a group that has the characteristics of a CoP. According to researchers Etienne Wenger, Richard McDermott, and William Snyder, the term *communities of practice* refers to an age-old pattern of individuals sharing their knowledge with others. This behavior has its roots in times when cave-dwelling humans met to determine the best ways to hunt their prey or which plants to eat. Researchers Jean Lave and Etienne Wenger agree that CoPs have existed for as long as people have been learning and sharing their experiences through storytelling. For example, generations of women have grouped together to pass down their knowledge of how to design, piece, and sew quilts. In a more modern context, Wenger, McDermott, and Snyder explain that engineers who debate over how to design a circuit, soccer moms who exchange tips about parenting, gang members who learn to survive the streets together, and manufacturing managers who commiserate about technologies and plan together for the future are all examples of informal CoPs that occur in everyday life.

Researchers including Lave and Wenger, John Brown and Paul Duguid, and Patricia Wesley and Virginia Buysse first used the formal concept of CoPs to describe how different occupational groups, such as architects and physicians, reflect on and improve their individual practices within their professions. The first CoPs emerged from a common desire among people with similar jobs to regularly reflect on and improve existing practices. According to studies by Carol Englert and Kathi Tarrant, Stephanie Pace Marshall and Connie Hatcher, and Patricia Wesley and Virginia Buysse, these original groups sought to develop common resources that each member could use in her own professional work, to challenge or support assumptions about certain practices, and to develop a shared worldview. These continue to be the main purposes of CoPs. Simply put, a CoP is a group of people who come together to problem-solve and reflect on real-life professional challenges, hot topics, or common interests by sharing experiences, ideas, tools, and resources.

## Why Join a CoP?

### Personal and Professional Benefits

CoPs can help strengthen teamwork, reduce feelings of professional isolation, improve professional practice, and provide personal growth for members, as researchers Karen McCreesh, Louise Larkin, and Jeremy Lewis explain. More specifically, researchers Melanie Barwick, Julia

Peters, and Katherine Boydell have found that CoP members gain a forum for exchanging knowledge and problem-solving collaboratively within real-life experiences. In a study by Torrey Trust and Brian Horrocks, education professionals who joined a CoP were more motivated and felt more confident in implementing new classroom practices. The ideal CoP, according to Wesley and Buysse, achieves these results because it incorporates the diverse expertise of its members and brings together research, policy, and practices in a way that is both meaningful and relevant to all members—something that is almost impossible to achieve through more-contrived, one-dimensional approaches, such as large-group training sessions or recorded webinars. Ultimately, collaborative reflection and inquiry-based dialogue are the true benefits of a CoP.

## Advantages over Traditional Professional Development

Often professional learning happens within our organizational contexts, such as with colleagues within our current buildings or organizations or with individuals who have job titles or roles similar to ours. The structures of professional learning also continue to include large-group training sessions, which by themselves will not result in practice change. In fact, research by Ruth Wei and her colleagues and by Carl Dunst has demonstrated that a person needs fifty hours or more of traditional professional development to effectively change a practice. Additionally, traditional professional development is often mandated by leadership or other organizational structures, so individuals do not get to pursue topics of interest or additional learning of their choice.

As Wesley and Buysse note, CoPs transcend organizational barriers by allowing professionals from various roles, geographic locations, and contexts to come together based on common interests, passions, or issues and to have additional time to apply and master new ideas or practices. In some instances, a CoP develops to solve a particular problem or to pursue a specific solution. At other times, a CoP may form based on the needs of professionals who identify a shared interest, seek support to address a challenge, or desire to engage in ongoing discussion about a specific topic. Either way, the nature of CoPs is evolving and organic, which creates the opportunity for extended learning for the members. The flexibility within a CoP allows extensive professional growth to occur.

## High Effectiveness and Low Cost

CoPs can be an essential component of ongoing learning for professionals who seek more than a “sit-and-get” professional-development opportunity. As researcher Carl Dunst writes both in his own article and in another coauthored with Carol Trivette, the traditional lecture-style method of training people in a workshop, conference session, or full-day training does not lead to effective changes in practice. These methods can effectively disseminate information to a large group, but they do not offer some critical components needed for people to really incorporate and use the new knowledge. Dunst and Trivette have researched professional development in early childhood intervention and have found that for an individual to actually change her practices in the long term, she needs job-embedded—or, as Sally Zepeda explains in an Education World article, on-the-job—opportunities to practice new skills, get feedback, and self-evaluate. Let’s look at an example of how this works.

### Case Study: Abby Learns on the Job

New preschool teacher Abby asks her colleague Jayla, a more experienced teacher, to observe in her (Abby's) room as Abby sets up and runs learning centers. Afterwards, Abby and Jayla meet privately. Abby shares her thoughts on how the observation went, and then Jayla offers her own thoughts and suggestions for improvement. A few weeks later, they repeat the observation and discussion to see how Abby's behavior or approach has changed. These types of opportunities to try new techniques in the classroom and to get real-time feedback are key to ensuring that individuals master improved practices.

The challenge, then, becomes determining how to provide job-embedded opportunities for experimentation and feedback. Some early childhood professionals may choose mentoring or coaching, which are extremely effective methods of helping individuals adopt or improve practices. However, each mentor or coach can only work with a small number of people, so if mentors and coaches are not an existing part of an organization and therefore require additional funding, these professional-learning methods can be cost prohibitive. CoPs, on the other hand, can offer support to many individuals at the same time, and their costs can be minimized by leveraging existing resources, such as having existing employees or volunteers serve as facilitators, using meeting spaces or conference-call lines that are already available, or adding CoP-related activities to regularly scheduled meetings. CoPs can also offer many naturally occurring opportunities to get and give feedback and to share resources, tips, and ideas that are "just in time," meaning that a professional can immediately apply that information in her individual practice to address a current problem or situation.

CoPs can effectively complement traditional professional development, but they are often overlooked, particularly in the early childhood field. Through this book, we hope to change that.

## How Are CoPs Different from Professional Learning Communities?

At this point, you might ask how CoPs are different from other professional-learning opportunities in which you may have participated. For example, professional learning communities (PLCs) and CoPs are sometimes confused because both groups share information, knowledge, and experience through formal structures, such as team meetings, group dialogue, protocols, or even virtual workspaces. The organizational culture in both types of communities is one of shared vision, with an emphasis on collaboration and trust. However, CoPs and PLCs have critical differences that are important to understand. While both group types have value, they offer practitioners different types of support and learning.

| Group Type | Structure | Organizational Culture | Membership | Purpose | Leadership | Knowledge Sharing |
|---|---|---|---|---|---|---|
| **Communities of Practice (CoPs)** | Team meetings, group dialogue, and virtual workspaces<br>Informal structure<br>Topics, agendas, and frequencies and lengths of meetings set by members | Shared vision<br>Emphasis on collaboration and trust | Voluntary<br>Members share passion, interest, or real-life issue | Improving group members' practices and learning | Formal and informal leaders within CoP | Valued<br>Learning through interaction<br>Members access, create, and share knowledge within CoP |
| **Professional Learning Communities (PLCs)** | Team meetings, group dialogue, and virtual workspaces<br>Formal structure<br>Topics, agendas, and frequencies and lengths of meetings set by administrators based on administrative plans | Shared vision<br>Emphasis on collaboration and trust<br>Members implement same practices outside PLC and report on experiences | Mandatory<br>Often includes an entire school, child-care center, or school district | Meeting student needs<br>Improving student achievement | Principal<br>School administrator | Limited<br>Collaboration<br>No in-depth discussion of how teams create and share new knowledge |

## How a PLC Works

As researchers Selena Blankenship and Wendy Ruona explain, a PLC is an approach to school improvement instituted by a principal, other administrators, monitors, or a school-wide leadership team. The membership of a PLC includes an entire organization, such as everyone who works in a particular school, department, or district. A PLC focuses on addressing student needs and achievement. The PLC's leadership chooses what the group will study by examining student-achievement data and identifying specific standards for which students are not meeting benchmarks. In an article for Education World, Celine Provini notes that a PLC typically uses a defined step-by-step process to improve outcomes.

The PLC approach is a long-term proposition and often takes three to six years to fully incorporate into a program environment. According to Provini, this approach functions best with widespread staff support and often benefits from having an external facilitator who is not also a member of the PLC. This person is usually someone from outside the program environment, though she could also be an administrator or lead teacher. PLC members frequently have a shared mission and values that drive the work, and they use collaborative processes aimed at improving student outcomes. But Blankenship and Ruona indicate that knowledge sharing, a key component of CoPs, is limited in a PLC, which focuses more on getting a group of people to adopt a certain way of thinking or doing things.

### Case Study: A PLC on Formative Assessment

One of the authors helped facilitate a PLC for which she and the other external facilitators decided on formative assessment as their topic. They then recruited members whose supervisors had already told them that they needed to improve their practices in this area. While the PLC participants chose what subtopics they wanted to cover within formative assessment, the external facilitators determined the scope of each discussion, what supporting documents and resources to share, and how long the PLC would last. Additionally, the knowledge sharing often went in only one direction, from facilitators or presenters to participants, rather than back and forth between them or among the participants.

## How a CoP Works

CoPs focus on expanding the learning and improving the practices of individuals rather than on meeting larger organizational-improvement goals. Blankenship and Ruona assert that membership in a CoP is always voluntary and happens organically, with leadership coming from within the group rather than from external facilitators. The Rhode Island Board of Regents for Elementary and Secondary Education (hereafter the RI Board of Regents) notes that CoPs provide safe and supportive spaces for professionals to share resources and ideas, explore and question their own understandings, solve challenges, and make shared commitments to improve. CoPs are more dynamic than PLCs because the membership and area of study in a CoP may fluctuate based on individuals' interests and needs for group support. Blankenship and Ruona add that CoPs are more likely than PLCs to build trusting relationships among their members that lead them to share knowledge and innovate. Instead of uniting the members behind a predetermined method or philosophy, a CoP encourages them to pool their expertise to discover what works best for them as individuals.

Importantly, CoPs can provide members with needed professional development that does not fit into organizational-improvement plans. CoPs typically meet outside the workplace, so they do not "steal" work time meant for pursuing improvement plans, and they do not need to report the results of members' participation to administrators or others outside the group. This is not to say that accountability within a program is a bad thing. Indeed, accountability moves a program as a whole toward improvement, and PLCs serve this important purpose. However, accountability often limits exploration and creativity, because people fear what might happen if they "waste" time by examining options and trying new ones and then fail to meet expectations. Given their light or nonexistent accountability requirements, CoPs provide a low-risk environment where members can freely explore and experiment with new practices until they find what works best for them and for the children and families they serve.

### Case Study: Pursuing Organizational and Individual Improvement

The program-improvement plan at ABC Early Learning Center includes multiple goals, most importantly a goal to increase children's kindergarten readiness. This goal mandates that all teachers use a certain approach to early literacy, so the center director forms a PLC to help the teachers become proficient in this method. Gabrielle, a toddler teacher, supports this goal but also wants to improve the effectiveness of transitions in her classroom. Several other teachers express similar concerns. However, PLC meetings take up all on-the-job professional-learning time at the center, and the director is unwilling to adjust the schedule to devote time to a topic that does not directly relate to the kindergarten-readiness goal.

As Gabrielle searches for another way to get support for improving her transitions, she discovers a local CoP with this shared interest. She joins the group, where she finds ideas and support from fellow teachers for managing transitions. In this setting, everyone can consider factors specific to individual situations, such as the children in Gabrielle's classroom, the expectations of her program, and her own beliefs about how transitions should work. Gabrielle explores all these issues in depth with other CoP members, who then share ideas and suggestions tailored to her circumstances. By participating in both the PLC and the CoP, she progresses toward her individual professional goals *and* her organization's program-improvement goals.

## Examples of CoPs across Sectors

CoPs have been used in a variety of professions besides education, such as business, public health, and social services. These groups provide examples of effectively used CoPs and offer ideas for using CoPs within the early childhood field.

### Business

Christopher Pappas, writing for eLearning Industry, states that in the business world, CoPs are created to improve performance and encourage innovative thinking through collaboration and expertise sharing. These CoPs provide mechanisms for innovating, reducing the learning curve for new staff, creating social capital, and adding organizational value, according to researchers Eric Lesser and John Storck. CoPs help develop new strategies and solve company- or industry-wide challenges. They also, as Pappas points out, allow every member to expand her professional knowledge to maximize productivity. The business world demonstrates how CoPs can address common, immediate, everyday challenges.

#### CoP Benefits Demonstrated by Business CoPs

- Addressing common, immediate, everyday challenges
- Strategically managing knowledge
- Reducing the learning curve for new staff
- Expanding professional knowledge

The following is an example of a CoP used in the business sector, quoted from the *Harvard Business Review* article "Communities of Practice: The Organizational Frontier" by Etienne Wenger and William Snyder.

### Case Study: Hewlett-Packard's CoP

> [At Hewlett-Packard,] a community of practice consisting of product-delivery consultants from around North America holds monthly teleconferences. The community focuses on an HP software product called High Availability, which minimizes computer downtime for customers. The core group of consultants, who had been somewhat isolated, came together a few years ago with the help of facilitators from a knowledge-management support team. The members discovered that they had many problems in common and that they could learn a great deal from one another. The community has succeeded in standardizing the software's sales and installation processes and establishing a consistent pricing scheme for HP salespeople.
>
> Participation in the monthly calls is voluntary, but levels of attendance are steady. For one such call, the focus was meant to be on Maureen's experiences with a major customer for which she was installing the product. . . .
>
> Maureen hadn't spent a lot of time preparing a formal presentation; she knew that only by talking directly and openly could she spur the give-and-take that would make the call worthwhile for the group. As the call proceeded, community members interrupted her constantly with questions and examples from their own experiences—all of which helped Maureen understand how to work more effectively with her clients.

Wenger and Snyder conclude that participants in this CoP learn from each other by concentrating on issues that directly relate to their work. As a result, the CoP members become more effective individually while creating a set of shared practices that are critical to the corporation's continuing success.

## Health Care

The article "How and Why Are Communities of Practice Established in the Health-Care Sector?" by Geetha Ranmuthugala and her colleagues explains that CoPs are used in health care as a means of learning and sharing knowledge and information, changing clinical practices with patients and promoting the use of best research evidence in these practices, and improving organizational performance. In their report *Communities of Practice in the Health Sector*, Ranmuthugala and her colleagues point out that because of the rapid knowledge advancement in the health-care field, many organizations establish CoPs to quickly integrate new practices, improve patient safety, and prevent adverse events. Health-care CoPs demonstrate that it is critical to leverage others' best practices through strong collaboration and sharing. Because CoPs offer many opportunities for feedback and mentoring, these groups can provide an effective, efficient way for professionals to master new and evolving practices.

### CoP Benefits Demonstrated by Health-Care CoPs

- Leveraging best practices through collaboration
- Promoting knowledge sharing and knowledge creation across disciplines
- Integrating practices effectively, efficiently, and with support

The following is an example of a CoP used in health care, paraphrased from the article "Thinking Together" by Igor Pyrko, Viktor Dörfler, and Colin Eden.

### Case Study: National Health Service Scotland's CoP

In one hospital of the National Health Service Scotland, the Critical Care Outreach Team, or Outreach Team, recognized a need to help all practitioners better diagnose and treat sepsis, a potentially life-threatening condition that any patient can develop. Though they never formally set up a group, the Outreach Team effectively used a CoP approach to change practices. They showed practitioners how to deal with actual cases of sepsis, mentored junior doctors and junior nurses, organized training courses about sepsis, and convened interdisciplinary meetings to discuss sepsis-related patient cases. The Outreach Team also designed objects to support interdisciplinary communication about sepsis, such as small card sets with key definitions, descriptions of symptoms, and required actions.

Through the Outreach Team's efforts, practitioners from across the hospital became interested in sepsis because they realized that it could strike their patients in the most unexpected moments. As a result, these professionals genuinely cared about various real-life problems surrounding sepsis and were willing to invest their time in learning more about it.

## Mental Health and Social Work

In the mental-health and social-work fields, CoPs aspire to reduce the stigma associated with mental illness, retain staff in the field, raise standards of treatment, and improve client care. CoPs in these disciplines offer opportunities for practitioners to share concerns, exchange views about patient treatment, and explore collaborative efforts to improve practice. The Social Service Institute adds that members of these CoPs sharpen their skills, develop bodies of knowledge to benefit their fields, share great ideas, and reflect on practices. Mental-health and social-work CoPs demonstrate the importance of reflection, and they provide examples of how to support both new and experienced practitioners within a field of study.

### CoP Benefits Demonstrated by Mental-Health and Social-Work CoPs

- Reflecting on the effectiveness of practices
- Improving the skills of practitioners with various experience levels

The following is an example of a CoP used in mental health, paraphrased from the article "Recovery Communities of Practice" by Myra Piat and her colleagues, published in the journal *Psychiatric Services*.

### Case Study: Quebec's Mental-Health CoP

In the city of Quebec, Canada, a group of managers, service users, practitioners, and researchers formed a CoP in 2012 to help people with mental illness. The CoP seeks to help its members collaborate, exchange knowledge, advocate for change, use a variety of strategies, and improve their practices. Today, the members meet each month to discuss risk management, various services and their levels of quality, how colleagues affect decisions about organizations and patients, and other relevant topics. The more members learn, the more they want to apply their discoveries to their own practices.

## Education

Etienne Wenger-Trayner and Beverly Wenger-Trayner are two of the leading experts in the science and use of CoPs. In their article "Introduction to Communities of Practice," they state that CoPs in education began as a method to support teacher training and peer-to-peer professional development and to provide isolated administrators with access to colleagues. CoPs have been used across educational sectors, particularly in special education. For instance, the Early Childhood Technical Assistance (ECTA) Center uses CoPs, which it calls *learning communities*, to address topics related to measuring outcomes and other early childhood subjects.

Visit http://ectacenter.org/resources/communities.asp to learn more about the ECTA Center's use of CoPs.

In most cases, CoPs are used to respond to the quickly changing educational landscape, such as by helping educators implement new evidence-based practices, use systemic-improvement planning (whether at the program level or the state level) in special education, or meet higher requirements for accountability and data collection. At all levels of education, CoPs demonstrate that there is an almost constant need in this field to address challenging situations and implement new practices. CoPs are effective mechanisms to create relationships among colleagues and to address a myriad of topics within a field of study.

### CoP Benefits Demonstrated by Education CoPs

- Quickly responding to new requirements or initiatives
- Establishing relationships among colleagues
- Addressing multiple topics within a field of study

This example of a CoP used in education is paraphrased from the research brief *Communities of Practice* by the National Council of Teachers of English.

### Case Study: English-Teacher CoP

English teachers must frequently give students feedback on their writing. In this CoP, several English teachers from the same middle school discuss what sorts of comments they write on students' papers. They realize that when encouraging students to develop their ideas, some teachers tend to use fairly broad suggestions, such as "Why?" or "Tell me more." The teachers decide to set a shared goal of customizing their feedback to individual papers or students. The next time they meet, they bring in commented-on papers and subsequent drafts that their students wrote after receiving those comments. These comparisons help the teachers discover how to use formative assessment to increase the quality of students' writing. The CoP also helps these teachers gain the necessary background knowledge to contribute to national, state, and local discussions on writing assessment.

## Overview of CoPs in Early Childhood Education

Now that we have seen how CoPs are used across sectors, including in education in general, let's begin exploring how you can use a CoP in the early childhood field. Professionals at all levels of the early childhood system—including classroom teachers; program administrators; specialists (such as early intervention providers, special educators, and speech, physical, and occupational therapists); regional or district leadership; and state early childhood, early intervention, or early childhood special-education leadership—can benefit from participating in CoPs. CoPs can help grow the professionalism, knowledge, and skills of all early childhood practitioners and thus elevate the status of the entire field.

### Design Principles

Wenger, McDermott, and Snyder have identified seven design principles that, when followed, bring out a CoP's direction, character, and energy and make CoPs successful in changing the practices of participants. These principles are as follows:

- **Design for evolution:** Set up the CoP's structure, policies, and practices in a way that encourages the CoP to continuously evolve according to members' interests and needs.
- **Foster open dialogue between inside and outside perspectives:** Invite contributions to the group's learning from both members and outside sources, such as books or expert presenters.
- **Invite different levels of participation:** Provide various ways for members to participate in and contribute to the group, whether regularly or occasionally.
- **Develop both public and private community spaces:** Use the strength of individual members' relationships to enrich CoP events, and use CoP events to strengthen individual members' relationships.
- **Focus on value:** Create events, activities, and relationships that provide recognizable value, such as support for current needs or contributions to a body of knowledge, to members. See chapters 5 and 6 for more about assessing a CoP's value.
- **Combine familiarity with excitement:** Build a safe space for members to ask for candid advice, share opinions, and try out new ideas. At the same time, plan various interesting events to introduce new ideas to the group, encourage discussion, maintain excitement, and promote professional growth.
- **Create a rhythm for the community:** Use a combination of whole-community and small-group gatherings to create balance between the thrill of exposure to many different ideas and the comfort of more-intimate relationships.

### Structural Components

In "Introduction to Communities of Practice," Wenger-Trayner and Wenger-Trayner identify three key structural components of successful CoPs:

- Domain
- Community
- Practice

The Edmonton Regional Learning Consortium provides specific definitions for each component. For a CoP, the *domain* is "the general area of interest" (note the difference from domains in early childhood pedagogy, such as social-emotional development). Wenger, McDermott, and Snyder further define a domain as the combination of a knowledge base, or broad topic, and a shared interest within that knowledge base. The Edmonton Regional Learning Consortium goes on to say that the *community* is a group of people who "pursue this interest through joint activities, discussions, problem-solving opportunities, information sharing, and relationship building." The *practice* is "the specific focus around which the community develops, shares, and maintains its core of collective knowledge." We explore these three components in detail throughout this book.

## Sample Early Childhood CoPs

In the early childhood field around the world, CoPs are often used as an alternative or an enhancement to traditional professional-development offerings. These CoPs include people who interact regularly, face corresponding concerns or issues, and share a passion for early childhood education. They offer each other a variety of supports, engage in discussions, and exchange information. Let's look at some examples.

### Case Study: The National Early Childhood Development Community of Practice

In South Africa, the National Early Childhood Development (ECD) Community of Practice began in 2013 because the country's ECD field needed a strong coordinating mechanism to bring together diverse stakeholders to collectively improve systems, according to the website of educational nonprofit organization BRIDGE. This CoP has grown to include approximately 650 members across all nine provinces of South Africa. As a result of the widespread sharing of knowledge at all levels, the CoP is making a significant contribution to the development of a strong and effective ECD system. BRIDGE's website quotes one participant: "'The CoP has connected me with organisations whose work complements our core work but adds a different dimension (such as a focus on early learning barriers) [that] we need in our programmes.'" The National ECD CoP is larger than most CoPs, but because the group focuses on improving early childhood across an entire nation, this CoP is an effective mechanism for creating a community across a large population of professionals.

Other CoPs in early childhood are smaller and more focused. The following two examples illustrate this type of CoP.

### Case Study: DaSy

In the United States, sections of the Individuals with Disabilities Education Act (IDEA) set out standards for special-education and early intervention professionals who work with young children. The Center for IDEA Early Childhood Data Systems (DaSy) offers CoPs where these providers can share lessons learned and promising practices in early intervention and preschool special-education data and data systems. Through these CoPs, DaSy engages state leaders, provides expert facilitation, and develops resources that benefit both the CoP participants and other professionals who face similar challenges.

Each DaSy CoP has ten to thirty members. This size provides an opportunity for the participants to delve deeply into topics of interest. For example, the Data Visualization CoP has thoroughly explored many low- or no-cost tools to create different ways of charting or graphing data based on audience and data type.

### Case Study: The Early Learning Leadership Initiative

In 2013, the US state of Delaware used a CoP framework to form the Early Learning Leadership Initiative (ELLI). This initiative provided participating early childhood educators with enhanced learning experiences and support to earn the national director credential as part of the state's Quality Rating and Improvement System (QRIS). Participants throughout the state met monthly and face-to-face for nine months to enhance the learning experience and complete the requirements for the credential, as Maria Edgerton of the McCormick Center for Early Childhood Leadership reports. As a result, the participants created a community of individuals with similar jobs who would otherwise be isolated and not easily able to share ideas, ask for help, or collaborate on critical daily issues. The ability to do these things with others who "get it" is invaluable to those who participate in any CoP.

### Feedback from an ELLI Participant

"I had no idea how beneficial the ELLI meetings would be. . . . It was so nice to be with people who could relate and truly understand the same daily challenges I face. The interactions with other directors were priceless. These meetings impacted me so much that I asked if anyone else in the group wished to continue our monthly meetings. Thankfully . . . one hundred percent of the class agreed to continue to meet. I am looking forward to continuing my relationships with my professional peers!"

—Heather Wilson, director of Brandywine Valley Christian Preschool and Kindergarten, quoted in *Communities of Practice: A Glimpse into Delaware* by Maria Edgerton

## Chapter 1 Study Guide

Based on the definitions and information about CoPs and PLCs that have been presented so far, what CoPs and/or PLCs have you participated in?

What were the outcomes of each group? the benefits? the challenges?

If you have participated in both PLCs and CoPs, what differences did you notice between them?

CHAPTER 2

# CREATING A COMMUNITY OF PRACTICE

### Case Study: An Unexpected CoP

The last session of the 2009 Division for Early Childhood (DEC) conference on exceptional children took place on a crisp, beautiful October day, the type when everyone would rather not be inside. But to the surprise of the facilitators (including one of the authors), early intervention professionals, early childhood special-education teachers, technical-assistance providers, trainers, and administrators crowded into the room. Soon there was standing room only.

Almost immediately, the participants actively began asking questions and answering those of their peers. It became clear that despite their varying roles, they had some important things in common. First, they all were seeking cost-effective ways to provide professional development for large numbers of early intervention and early childhood special-education professionals. Second, many participants expressed concerns about limited resources and their own inability to develop the materials they needed. Third, the attendees all wanted to avoid reinventing the wheel if someone had already developed materials that they could use. At this time, online learning was a relatively new trend in professional development, and it quickly became the focus of the discussion.

> Visit http://eieconlinelearning.pbworks.com/w/page/47454169/New%20to%20the%20EI-EC%20PD%20CoP to learn more about the EI–EC PD CoP.

As the one-hour session wound down, the facilitators recognized that the group had only scratched the surface of this topic and that the participants would benefit tremendously from continuing to address this shared interest together. The facilitators proposed an opportunity for the conversation to continue outside of the conference. Though the participants came from all across the United States and no one really knew how this continued conversation might work, most attendees replied, "Yes, please!" The facilitators quickly passed around a pen and paper and asked interested people to list their contact information. Within a few weeks, a CoP was born.

A decade later, the members of this CoP still share time, expertise, and resources to jointly develop tools and materials to support online learning in the field of early childhood intervention. Subgroups have evolved as certain interests have led small groups to explore more-specific tasks and activities. What began as a single conference session has evolved into the Early Intervention–Early Childhood Professional Development Community of Practice (EI–EC PD CoP).

## Developing a Shared Interest

This chapter looks at the big picture of starting a CoP. Much as with the CoP in the opening story, the process includes these steps:

1. Identifying a shared interest to explore (in this case, online learning and the use of technology for professional development)
2. Articulating a shared practice connected to that interest (here, creating online professional development while maximizing knowledge and resources)
3. Finding potential members of the community (in this case, the session participants)
4. Setting up parameters for the CoP (such as how members will join and how to orient new members)

This chapter also details some successes and challenges you may encounter in the early stages of setting up a CoP.

### Natural Opportunities to Connect over a Shared Interest

Perhaps you can empathize with the people in the opening story and the feeling of wanting more from a professional-development experience. Perhaps you have even exchanged contact information with someone you met in a training session so you could continue a conversation about what you learned. Consider for a moment your knowledge base in your area of early childhood as well as your interests, strengths, challenges, and problems. Might your counterparts in your specific area of expertise have these things in common with you? Could your teammates in other roles also share these concerns, regardless of their professional disciplines, backgrounds, and levels of experience? Chances are that some things are unique to you and some are shared by other professionals, perhaps even within your professional partnerships with families.

Now consider what formal and informal opportunities you have to connect with others about such issues. A formal opportunity, for example, could be attending a training session or completing continuing-education coursework. An informal opportunity might be seeking out a coworker, mentor, or supervisor to discuss your interests, experiences, and practices. You might gravitate toward other professionals in your discipline or those who perform similar duties to yours. Or perhaps you seek out people who have or are looking for answers to your own questions, regardless of those people's professional roles.

Early childhood professionals have many natural opportunities to find others who want to learn more about a certain interest, knowledge base, or set of practices. For example, child-care providers across the United States are participating in Quality Rating and Improvement System (QRIS) processes or pursuing accreditation through the National Association for the Education of Young Children (NAEYC). Early interventionists are implementing reflective coaching, the primary service provider approach, or routines-based intervention. Early childhood special-education program leaders are beginning to use the Pyramid Model for Promoting Social-Emotional Competence in Infants and Young Children. Regional technical-assistance providers are implementing systems coaching and other types of professional development across their states. Each of these initiatives is a knowledge base that early childhood professionals could share an interest in and select for further exploration as they work to improve their practices.

## The Importance of Commitment to a Shared Interest

Your informal or formal opportunities to connect with others may already include some elements of shared interests, community, practice, or all three. However, people can have knowledge, interests, and challenges in common and still not a desire to change practices or to rely on a community of supports to help you achieve something more. A CoP does not exist unless group members commit to the shared interest and seek more for their practices than just a simple solution to a problem. According to Wenger, McDermott, and Snyder, a domain (the combination of a knowledge base and a shared interest) is not a fixed set of problems but rather something that evolves with the community and the ever-changing needs of its members. The shared interest is what gives the community its identity, holds members accountable, and inspires individuals to prioritize their connections and involvement with the community.

Wenger, McDermott, and Snyder imply that without commitment to the shared interest or to the desire to develop new knowledge or practices, a group is not a CoP but simply a network of friends, peers, or colleagues. For example, if the people in the opening story had simply kept in contact after the conference to occasionally discuss professional development or how to use technology to carry it out, they would have created a simple network based on their shared interest. Instead, these members formed a CoP by committing to a higher level of involvement: they agreed to learn from one another, share ideas, and collaborate in ways that would help them improve their practices.

Let's look at some other examples that help us differentiate between a CoP and a network. In our personal and professional lives, we often share interests or a knowledge base with people we interact with. From time to time, we seek out peers, supervisors, or subject-matter experts to find help with issues related to our shared knowledge base or interests. For instance, Ed, who teaches four-year-olds, has a student who screams at the slightest provocation, despite Ed's best efforts to address this behavior. Ed asks for advice from his coworkers, his director, and one of his former college professors. To varying degrees, all these people share a knowledge base (young children's behavior) and an interest (Ed's and his students' well-being) with Ed. However, if Ed merely seeks and gains support from this group to address his current problem, rather than working with them regularly so that they all learn more about challenging behavior and develop better practices to address it, then these people may simply be part of his network of supports rather than a true CoP. Networks of support are important, but they do not include all the elements of a CoP (shared interest, sense of community, and desire to expand knowledge and improve practices).

### Case Study: One Person's Network Is Another Person's CoP

Daniela, Marcos, and several other preschool teachers are learning how to collect important data to track child-outcome measures and how to enter that information into a database used for state and federal reporting purposes. As they learn and practice together, the teachers discuss knowledge, interests, and challenges they have in common. They become a network of supports for each other, helping each other troubleshoot when they get stuck.

Once the group members have learned the technical skills they need to collect and enter the data, Marcos is ready to move on. For him, this network of supports has served its purpose—helping him learn how to gather and record certain types of data—and may even be available to answer more questions if they arise. But because Marcos does not have any desire to learn or develop additional knowledge, skills, or practices, the group does not necessarily provide him with an ongoing, professional-growth-seeking community of like-minded individuals.

However, Daniela and a few others in this network learn that they share other interests related to child outcomes, such as how to use the collected data to inform and transform their practices. These people commit to engage together in further activities that will help them learn more about making data-informed decisions and applying this knowledge to their practices. For Daniela and her new colleagues, this network of supports could evolve into a CoP.

## Establishing a Shared Interest

A CoP can establish its shared interests in numerous ways. In some instances, as Wenger, McDermott, and Snyder note, this happens spontaneously when a group of peers, colleagues, or professionals connect and recognize that they can help one another learn and improve their practices by keeping their conversations going. This type of event could happen at a staff meeting, an all-organization meeting, a local professional-development opportunity, a statewide or national conference—essentially, anywhere professionals can come together in person or online.

In other instances—as noted by Line Dubé, Anne Bourhis, and Réal Jacob and by Wenger, McDermott, and Snyder—an individual or an organization may intentionally form a CoP to address a problem or pursue an organizational goal. This type of CoP can evolve into much more if members find individual value in the shared interests and practices they develop together. In their report *Promoting and Assessing Value Creation in Communities and Networks*, Etienne Wenger, Beverly Trayner, and Maarten de Laat assert that "there can be short-term value in solving problems that members have in their [practices], but over time, the approaches and solutions to these challenges become a cumulative resource for members facing new challenges, both individually and collectively." Once they have achieved their original goal, the CoP members can revisit their interests and decide whether they would like to dissolve the CoP or explore a new set of shared interests and practices. The following example illustrates how this can happen.

### Case Study: Purpose Fulfilled—Now What?

A system-wide change in special education is on the horizon, so administrators, trainers, and technical-assistance providers create a CoP to bring stakeholders together and establish a plan for implementing the (fictional) Z Method, a new evidence-based practice that promotes inclusion. In this CoP, inclusion is the shared interest, and the Z Method is the practice.

Once the members have created an effective plan for incorporating the Z Method into various settings and situations, the CoP has fulfilled its original purpose. At this time, the members have a choice to make: they can stay connected and identify new interests and practices to explore together, or they can dissolve the CoP if they feel that their shared interest and commitment to the group are no longer priorities for them.

Several members report that they have found value in the knowledge and skills they have gained from their CoP participation. These members decide to continue their work together, now focusing on evaluating the effects of the changes they have made to incorporate the Z Method into their work. Their shared interest continues to be inclusion, but the practices they explore have evolved.

When a CoP forms, establishing the shared interest begins by posing some important questions (adapted from Wenger, McDermott, and Snyder) to everyone who wants to participate:

- What are our group's collective strengths, challenges, and problems?
- What topics and issues do we care about?
- How will this CoP benefit us individually?
- How might the people we serve and partner with, such as family members, caregivers, or other team members, benefit from our involvement in the CoP and our development of shared practices?
- How will this CoP benefit our individual organizations, systems, or programs?

Anyone can ask these questions of potential CoP members and see where it leads the discussion. This could take place during or after staff meetings, reflective-supervision sessions, peer reflections, focus groups, online forums, individual phone calls, conference calls, or professional-learning opportunities. Regardless of how it takes place, Wenger, Trayner, and de Laat explain that this conversation is a critical step in developing a CoP. If people do not understand what they will gain from their involvement in the CoP and how it aligns with their interests (and, in some instances, their organizations' interests), they will not commit to participation or eagerly take on any responsibilities in the CoP.

Remember that potential CoP members may come from within one organization or from multiple organizations spread out across a county, state or province, or nation. Potential members may also come from different disciplines across early childhood—such as teachers, service coordinators, higher-education faculty, researchers, supervisors, administrators, professional-development specialists, training and technical-assistance providers, and so on—yet all may share a knowledge base, interests, and practices. Given all these variations, methods for establishing shared interests will vary. The next several sections provide some ideas.

### Gathering Ideas by Testing Operational Styles

One way to help establish a shared interest is to kill two birds with one stone: gather ideas by testing operational styles for your CoP. As previously discussed, Wenger, McDermott, and Snyder explain that the process for establishing a CoP and its knowledge base, shared interests, and shared practices can be spontaneous or intentional. This process can suggest, though it does not dictate, whether a formal or informal operational style would work better for your CoP. A CoP that forms intentionally often takes a formal (highly structured) approach, such as having defined roles within the group, meetings with set agendas, and a website or workspace for members to share knowledge and resources. A CoP that forms spontaneously often structures itself more informally, such as by simply setting dates and times to talk about whatever is on members' minds.

Whether you favor one or the other operational style at the outset or are undecided, you can use strategies from either or both approaches to gather ideas for shared interests or practices. For example, after a professional-networking opportunity, you might take the informal approach of inviting potential CoP members to discuss their interests or problems over lunch or via an email thread. As you hear or read the responses, you can determine whether a shared knowledge base or interest already exists or whether the potential members need to do something more to establish common interests and practices to improve on. In contrast, you might take the formal approach of sending out an electronic survey or scheduling a focus group to find out what potential group members have in common and want to learn.

Whichever methods you use, the members' responses can also help you decide whether a formal or informal operational style will work best in your group. For instance, if an informal lunch discussion stalls because people do not know what to say, you might want to create formal agendas for future meetings to provide built-in discussion topics.

The following table—adapted from the work of Wenger, McDermott, and Snyder—compares CoPs that are spontaneous and informal with those that are intentional and formal.

| Formation Process | Operational Style | Sample Strategies for Determining Shared Interests or Practices |
|---|---|---|
| **Spontaneous:** members come together because they need each other as peers and learning partners, with no intervention or development effort from an organization | **Informal:** no set meeting schedule, no or loose agendas, no set methods of communication or formal structure in place to sustain the CoP | Inviting peers or colleagues to discuss their interests or problems over lunch or via an email thread |
| **Intentional:** organizations or people create specific communities to develop a needed capability | **Formal:** clearly defined roles, set meeting schedule and agendas, data-driven decisions, creating artifacts (such as websites, tools, and resources) with community branding or logo | Using a questionnaire or survey, coordinating a focus group, or facilitating a formal discussion |

The bottom line is that there is no right or wrong way to form or operate a CoP. Any combination of formation process and operational style can help you create an effective CoP and collect ideas to begin defining its shared interests and practices.

### Gathering Ideas through Technology

Advances in technology have made it easier for people to connect and gather information from one another that can help them establish shared interests and practices. Technology has also made it easier to build a CoP regardless of where the members live and work. Online formats and platforms, many of which are free, allow people to learn about and with one another.

Electronic surveys make it easy to gather information from any number of people at any time and across geographic and organizational boundaries, so they are especially useful for gathering information about shared interests. Some survey-building tools, such as SurveyMonkey, SurveyGizmo, or Google Forms, have free versions that anyone can access by signing up for an account. Surveys can also gather qualitative or quantitative data or both and provide reports that help you analyze the results, such as identifying commonly mentioned interests, desires, strengths, and challenges. For example, if you already know about some shared interests and priorities among potential group members, you can have respondents rank or choose from among those items on a survey.

Regardless of how you gather the information, reporting the overall results to the potential CoP members helps you check your understanding of the information you have received, seek additional clarity or detail, and identify additional potential members as the group's shared interests and practices crystallize.

### Settling on Shared Interests and Practices

Successful and sustainable CoPs have focused, well-defined purposes that directly tie to the members' priorities. Any number of shared interests and practices can exist in an early childhood CoP. The following list gives some examples:

- improving services for infants and toddlers in early intervention programs
- creating socially and emotionally supportive classrooms for four-year-olds
- enhancing instructional practices for children with autism

So how do you choose which shared interest or practice to focus on in your CoP? An organization or facilitator might take note of hot topics or systemic changes happening in the field and use that information to cultivate a list of possible shared interests. Ultimately, though, the CoP members—or potential members, if the CoP is just forming—will choose what interests them most and which practices they would like to explore together. When several related shared interests arise, the facilitator may need to narrow the list by asking follow-up questions.

### Case Study: Narrowing the Options

A group of administrators share an interest in developing their leadership practices and decide to form a CoP to explore this topic. They choose Yoshi as their facilitator. However, leadership is a broad category, so to decide what activities and topics the CoP should pursue, Yoshi needs to learn what the members want to know about leadership and what practices they seek to improve. He builds a list of possible meeting topics and emails the list to the other CoP members, asking each person to rank the topics in order of priority based on the specific leadership practices that that person seeks to develop. The members' responses will help him determine what the group's shared interest really is.

See chapter 5 for more about how to assess and evaluate CoPs when they form and as they evolve.

## Founding a Community around Shared Interests and Practices

CoPs often form out of existing networks of coworkers and colleagues and evolve along with the interests of the members. Regardless of how the idea arises to start a CoP, participants are needed to form the community component of the group—the *C* in *CoP*. This section examines key tasks needed to bring together the people who will make up the community.

### Helping Potential Members Find Value in the CoP

Wenger, McDermott, and Snyder state that people join CoPs for different reasons: some join primarily because of interest in a certain knowledge base, some for the sense of community, others for the opportunity for growth and development in their practices, and some for all of these reasons. The sense of community can be especially important. CenterPoint Institute comments that in an age of technology and globalization in which more and more people work remotely, the desire for community is (perhaps counterintuitively) becoming the standard rather than the exception in most workplaces. A community sometimes develops naturally among people who work in physical proximity to one another, such as in nearby offices. For people who work remotely, it is not always that easy, and a sense of community needs to be consciously fostered.

In recent years, advances in technology have made it much easier for people who work remotely to find a sense of community with people who share their interests and the desire to expand their knowledge bases and improve their practices. Google Hangouts, Zoom video-conference rooms, FaceTime, and Facebook Live are just a few ways that people can connect with and see each other, even if they do not live or work near one another. Still, it requires intentional action to get and stay connected with CoP members who participate from remote locations. See chapter 4 for some strategies that facilitators can use to foster engagement in these CoPs.

Within a CoP, all members need to find value in their participation. According to Wenger, Trayner, and de Laat as well as to Wenger, McDermott, and Snyder, value can be individualized or organizational. The following table provides some examples, some of which are adapted from Wenger, McDermott, and Snyder.

| Individualized Value | Organizational Value |
| --- | --- |
| Through the CoP's support, Odessa develops her skills in classroom management and thus grows as a professional. | Jamal, a preschool principal, notices that his employees always return from CoP meetings with new ideas, resources, and strategies that benefit the school. |
| Victor finds networking opportunities and develops relationships within the CoP that provide chances for social learning over time. | Queenie, a child-care-center director, and her CoP discuss how to implement a new set of state requirements for outdoor play areas, making the transition process much smoother than Queenie and her staff expected. |

As previously mentioned, there is no right or wrong way to set up or run a CoP. A CoP community that starts at the request of an administrator and has an appointed facilitator can be just as valuable as one created and led by group members. Sometimes the former type of group will start out to address a systemic or organizational goal and then evolve as members begin to develop relationships and a sense of common purpose beyond the initial objective.

Wenger, McDermott, and Snyder state that ideally, both individuals and organizations find value in CoPs, as the most successful communities are the ones where the goals and needs of an organization intersect with the passions and aspirations of the participants. Regardless, the value and benefits of membership must be clear to the potential members before the CoP begins meeting. You and other potential CoP leaders may want to explore how to articulate the value of participation so you can share it when reaching out to interested individuals.

## Establishing Leadership

By now, you might be wondering, "Who's going to be in charge of all this?" This book addresses the role of the facilitator in chapter 4. However, CoPs require some form of leadership at the outset, well before a facilitator is chosen, to bring individuals together around the shared interest or practices they have identified. This is where you come in!

There are many ways to acquire leaders for a CoP. The following list gives a few methods and examples.

- **A single leader emerges organically:** Preschool teacher Sheila decides to invite people who work in her building to routinely meet for lunch to connect and share practical strategies.
- **Shared leadership emerges organically:** Latoya, Chul-soon, and Itzel have been the primary drivers of the effort to establish a CoP in their city. Latoya has strong computer skills and volunteers to run the group's online workspace, Chul-soon takes excellent notes and agrees to act as secretary during meetings, and Itzel communicates well and therefore takes on the role of discussion leader.
- **Group members intentionally choose a leader from among themselves:** A CoP forms as teachers at Rolling Hills Preschool begin to video themselves in the classroom to reflect on their practices. Of the CoP members, Johanna has the most experience with this practice, as she has been using video for years. She knows all about the consent forms required to ensure privacy and confidentiality when using this technique, and she has tried several types of video cameras and other technologies to document her practices. Given Johanna's knowledge about and experience with this shared interest, her fellow members nominate her to help lead the CoP.
- **An external authority appoints a leader for the group:** A professional-development coordinator assigns Una to facilitate a CoP centered on teaching members how to use a new state-mandated curriculum.

In any case, the success of a CoP depends on the early identification of someone who has (a) the knowledge and skills to start conversations about the shared interests and practices, (b) the time to cultivate connections with current or future CoP members, and (c) some foundational knowledge about the shared interests of the CoP. Note that the facilitator does not have to be an expert on the shared interest or on the shared practices that the CoP members hope to develop, but it does help for him to have a basic understanding of these topics. One method that has worked well for the authors is to establish a core group of leadership as the CoP begins to form. Depending on the size or potential size of the CoP, this small unit could include two to five individuals who take on the initial leadership of the CoP. For instance, in a newly forming CoP that intends to reach professionals across an entire nation, the core group can make the initial decisions about setting up infrastructure, identifying the group's shared interests, and managing membership; later, they can establish the CoP's long-term leadership. In contrast, a small, informal, organically created CoP may be able manage with two leaders who can share perspectives and decide how to manage the group. (See chapter 4 for strategies for and benefits of using a team approach to CoP leadership.)

## Recruiting the Founding Members

In the early childhood field, a CoP may have members from many different roles who share interests, including early interventionists, special-education providers, teachers, and administrators. Regardless of specific job titles, it make sense to recruit individuals for a CoP who want to contribute to the group's knowledge base or to help the group contribute new information or solutions to problems in the field. In other words, seek members who can both benefit and be benefited by the CoP. For example, your colleague may be an excellent head cook at the child-care center where you both work, but he will probably have little to contribute to a CoP focused on early literacy assessments. Instead, you might want to recruit teachers and administrators from state-funded preschools, who will more likely be interested in and be able to contribute to the CoP's work.

Like CoP leaders, members might join a CoP by choice or by assignment. But because a useful and positive CoP experience depends on the members' passion, interests, and ability to identify with each other and to share their practice-related interests and successes, people should ideally have the freedom to join on their own rather than being coerced or mandated to participate. While participation can be encouraged, engagement should always be voluntary, as argued by Wenger, McDermott, and Snyder and by Blankenship and Ruona.

In any newly established CoP, if members join the group by assignment from their organizations, their participation will vary according to their personal interests. If an individual's interests and passions align with the shared interest of the CoP, he will likely engage in the group's activities. Otherwise, he will probably not actively participate. In their article "Levels of Participation," Etienne Wenger-Trayner and Beverly Wenger-Trayner argue that even among group members who participate voluntarily, share the group's interest, and have a strong desire to improve their practices, levels of participation will probably vary, with members moving in and out of the community as their needs dictate. For example, if an individual changes professional roles (such as being promoted from teacher to director) or if his priorities and responsibilities shift (such as getting a new student with special needs), his interests, the practices he seeks to develop, and his availability to participate may also change.

Alternatively, sometimes a CoP evolves into something that no longer provides value for an individual or an organization, such as if a CoP begins to study a curriculum that a participant's program does not use. Evolution within a CoP is a good thing; in fact, it is the first design principle identified by Wenger, McDermott, and Snyder. However, it can present challenges to membership maintenance and growth. For example, when new members join a CoP, it may take some time for relationships and trust to develop between new members and existing members. Because new members do not know what discussions and activities have already taken place, they might unwittingly cause the CoP to take steps back by reviving old topics or issues that distract everyone from current concerns. It may take time to bring the newcomers up to speed so that the CoP continues to move forward.

Of course, as membership grows, new members bring new knowledge, experiences, and problems to be solved, and the group's overall interests may evolve. This may signal a need to revisit—and, in some instances, reestablish—the CoP's shared interest and practices.

### Case Study: New Member, New Shared Interest?

Nicki facilitates a CoP that formed based on a shared interest in supporting early childhood professionals using technology and distance-learning opportunities. Tatiana, a doctoral student, recently joined the CoP and has been monopolizing meeting time as she seeks support for her research project on how, when, and why to use technology to support distance-learning opportunities. While this topic does relate to the CoP's shared interest, Nicki worries that Tatiana may steer the CoP away from its original purpose.

In this instance, Nicki needs to gauge the other members' responses to Tatiana's specific interest. If other members seem disengaged, remain quiet during discussions, and begin to excuse themselves from meetings, then Nicki needs to intervene and ensure that meetings stay focused on the CoP's overall shared interests and practices. She might suggest that those who want to continue discussing Tatiana's research could form a subgroup to explore this new shared interest.

Alternatively, if most or all members remain engaged in discussions, exchange ideas, and appear to benefit from Tatiana's specific interest, then Nicki may decide to simply see where things lead. It is fine for a CoP's shared interest to evolve, provided that that change continues to meet members' needs.

## Membership Parameters

When establishing a CoP, you and your fellow group members have to decide how to manage membership. There are three types of membership for a CoP: open, closed, and circumstantial. Each option has benefits and challenges, which are summarized in the following table. Each CoP must decide which type of membership works best for its situation.

| Type | Parameters | Benefits | Challenges | Tips |
|---|---|---|---|---|
| **Open Membership** | Continuously welcomes, invites, and recruits new members | New ideas and growth<br>Renewed energy<br>Fresh perspectives<br>New knowledge, skills, or expertise brought into CoP<br>Possible evolution and new connections and opportunities for members | Members need time to get to know one another and develop trust and relationships<br>New members must learn about past and present activities to avoid repetition or regression<br>Constant change can affect group's dynamics and ability to stay focused on shared interests and practices | Adopt new-member-orientation process to welcome and introduce new members to CoP (such as scheduling a phone call to orient newcomers before next full-group meeting)<br>Inform new members of tools used for engagement and communication (such as social-media platforms, online workspaces, or email lists)<br>Share archived meeting minutes with new members<br>Notify new members of topics previously discussed and of tools and resources already developed or shared |
| **Closed Membership** | Establishes membership at the formation of the group and does not welcome, invite, or recruit anyone new to join | No need for new-member-orientation practices<br>Consistent focus on members' shared interests and goals for their practices<br>Time for members to develop trust and relationships and really get to know one another | Group has no opportunities for new or fresh ideas<br>CoP risks growing stagnant or "suffocating itself" (Wenger, McDermott, and Snyder)<br>Interests and roles may change, diminishing the number of members<br>CoP risks dissolving | Rely on strong relationships among members<br>Be creative in methods of rejuvenating CoP (such as introducing new topics, inviting guest speakers, and even holding joint meetings with other CoPs) (Wenger, McDermott, and Snyder)<br>Be open to revisiting membership parameters as CoP evolves |
| **Circumstantial Membership** | Admits new members on a select basis<br>In some instances, requires approval from current members before anyone new can join | The benefits of open membership without the disruption of too many new members at once<br>Member ownership in CoP decisions via approval process, if used | CoP needs a process for welcoming in new people so shared interests and practices are not lost<br>CoP faces some risk of stagnation and extinction unless new members are actively recruited<br>Approval process, if used, can make joining CoP a lengthy process | Establish process for inviting & welcoming new members<br>If approval process exists, identify who takes part (such as the facilitator, the entire group, or a membership committee)<br>Be open to revisiting membership parameters and new-member procedures as CoP evolves |

### Open Membership

Open communities, which allow new members to join at any time, benefit from new ideas, fresh perspectives, and new knowledge and skill sets that can help the community evolve. Wenger, McDermott, and Snyder comment that these CoPs may also choose to actively recruit new members to continuously bring new ideas and life into the community. Active recruiting can happen through, for example, word of mouth, emails, focus groups, electronic surveys, newsletters, social media, presentations (such as at local, state, national, or international meetings or conferences), outreach to professional associations, or training and professional-development opportunities.

Whether or not they actively recruit, open CoPs must establish some practices for welcoming and orienting new members. This helps preserve the shared interest of the CoP, helps new members feel supported and included in ongoing activities, and ensures that the CoP is a good fit for the newcomers based on their roles, experiences, interests, and desired practices. You may want to establish a vetting process for potential members, perhaps including a series of questions that candidates must answer before they can join the CoP. Those questions could include the following:

- How did you learn about this CoP?
- What do you hope to gain from the CoP?
- What do you feel you bring to the CoP?

The vetting process could happen through phone calls, email correspondence, or, more formally, through short surveys or feedback forms that candidates can easily access on the CoP's website or online workspace.

One useful way to orient newly admitted members is to hold one-on-one or small-group meetings with them apart from the regularly scheduled CoP meetings. Spend some time learning more about how the newcomers found out about the CoP and what interests them most. Demonstrate the various ways in which CoP members engage with one another, such as online workspaces and social-media pages, and provide a list of in-person meeting dates. You can also use this time to review recent meeting minutes and show new members how and where to access information about the CoP's past and ongoing activities.

One disadvantage of open CoPs is that when new members continuously join, it can disrupt existing group dynamics. Sometimes a shakeup in group dynamics can breathe new life into a group that needs renewed energy. However, if new members receive inadequate support, they could temporarily set the CoP back by, for example, revisiting questions or agenda items that the group has already resolved. Furthermore, even if existing members have developed an elevated level of trust with one another, it may take some time for them to trust the new members. Similarly, it will take time for the newcomers to learn to trust the existing members. Thus, new and existing members alike may be guarded with their contributions to the group for some time.

Ultimately, each CoP needs to decide whether open membership works for its members. Should the community decide to be an open one, leaders and members will need to work together to establish specific membership parameters and new-member-orientation practices.

### Closed Membership

Despite the numerous benefits to having an open CoP, some communities feel more secure with closed membership. A closed CoP establishes membership at the beginning of the group, so the founding members are the only members. A closed CoP does not need to establish new-member-orientation practices, as it does not expect new members to join.

One benefit of a closed CoP, as noted by Wenger, McDermott, and Snyder, is that members can stay focused on their shared interests and objectives. Closed membership may suit a CoP that develops to help members collaborate on a specific goal, such as making organizational changes or implementing a new policy or procedure.

#### Case Study: A Case for Closed Membership

Like many early childhood programs in the United States, Meadowlark Child-Care Center receives funds from the federal government to serve children with disabilities. Therefore, as the Center for Early Childhood IDEA Data Systems (DaSy) points out, Meadowlark must follow the State Systemic Improvement Plan (SSIP) for its location. As part of these efforts, Meadowlark cultivates a CoP to help staff members identify their strengths, areas where they need support, and shared practices they need to learn.

In this example, Meadowlark's CoP might work best with closed membership so that relationships can blossom among the founding members as they get to know one another, learn about each other's skill sets, and establish a strong sense of trust among themselves. These bonds may improve their productivity and help them stay on task as they work toward the shared goals and practices connected to the SSIP.

According to Wenger, McDermott, and Snyder, the greatest risk a closed CoP faces is extinction. If the energy of the CoP wanes, if interests or organizational roles or responsibilities change, or if turnover occurs, the members may need to revisit their membership parameters. For example, members of a closed CoP might retire, get promotions that take them away from the CoP, or leave their positions and thus stop participating, resulting in dwindling membership and leaving the group at risk of dissolving. If the remaining members feel that the CoP has served its purpose, it may be an appropriate time for the group to end. However, if members still wish to collaborate on developing practices related to their initial shared interests, the CoP may need to revise its membership parameters to help add new life, expertise, and energy into the group. If the CoP decides to open to new members, it will need to establish new-membership-orientation practices and recruitment strategies. Alternatively, the existing members may choose to limit whom they invite, leading to the third type of membership for a CoP: circumstantial membership.

### Circumstantial Membership

CoPs with circumstantial membership are a mix between open and closed CoPs. These CoPs do not actively seek new members but may open their membership on a situational basis. A circumstantial CoP needs to establish a protocol for deciding who can join and when. The CoP leaders might make these decisions, or they might facilitate the process as the entire community decides.

### Case Study: Establishing Circumstantial Membership Parameters

The Blue Skies Child-Care Network develops a CoP to help its center directors learn practices to support teachers who are using Positive Behavior Supports (PBS) to address challenging behaviors in their classrooms. The CoP leaders invite all Blue Skies center directors to join the group as founding members. Because all members of this CoP need to share a certain knowledge base and interests, such as working in a supervisory role to support teachers who use PBS, this CoP is probably unsuitable for anyone who is not a director or who does not have experience with PBS. By establishing these circumstantial membership parameters up front, the CoP's leaders will have an easier time managing new membership requests, verifying potential members' credentials, and introducing new members into the CoP.

In some instances, circumstantial membership may require that CoP members have a voice in decisions about who can join. For example, a CoP might not actively recruit but may allow existing members to advocate for admitting new members who share the community's need for connection and desire to improve practices. These policies, in turn, require the CoP to have some procedures for vetting and approving new members. Whatever protocol a CoP decides to use for choosing new members, the group should consistently apply that protocol to all applications for membership.

### Case Study: Recruiting Keisha

Haluk belongs to a CoP focused on helping preschool teachers implement a new curriculum. At a conference, he meets Keisha, whose program began using the same curriculum a year earlier. Feeling that Keisha shares his CoP's vision and that her expertise could support the existing members, Haluk obtains Keisha's consent and submits a request for her to be admitted into his CoP.

At their next meeting, the CoP members considers Haluk's request, with facilitator Marisa moderating the discussion. Following CoP procedures for recommending new members, Haluk provides some background information on Keisha and shares some ways that she could add value to the CoP. Other existing members ask questions about Keisha. Finally, Marisa calls for a group vote on whether to welcome Keisha into the CoP. To Haluk's relief, the result is yes.

## Chapter 2 Study Guide

Consider your knowledge base, interests, strengths, and challenges, as well as any professional problems you wish to solve. What formal and informal opportunities do you have to connect with people who share these things? Are there organizations or networks that support these opportunities?

What do you seek in your professional sphere that a CoP could help you with? For example, are you looking for a chance to share knowledge, a sense of community, or a way to improve your or your organization's practices?

If you are a technical-assistance provider, trainer, or professional-development provider, consider the networking opportunities you facilitate and the feedback you gather through assessments or post-training evaluations. How might these activities help you identify opportunities to create a CoP?

Could you create time or space to connect with others and form a CoP so you can develop shared practices related to your or your organizations' shared interests? If so, list the steps you need to take to create that time or space.

List any technologies, tools, or resources you could explore to help you gather information from people who share your interests, want to develop similar practices, or both.

If you already belong to a CoP, what types of questions were you asked as you became part of that group? Were those questions asked electronically or in person?

If you are a facilitator or leader of a CoP or of a similarly structured group, what tools did you use to help establish the shared interests and practices of its members?

If you currently participate in a CoP or in a similarly structured group, what value do you get from your participation? What, if any, value does your organization get from your participation?

If you currently participate in a CoP, is your participation voluntary, or were you asked or assigned to represent your organization? How do you think this choice or lack thereof has affected your participation in the CoP?

If you currently participate in a CoP, is the membership open, closed, or circumstantial? What do you feel the benefits and disadvantages are for this type of membership?

If you are planning to develop or have recently developed a CoP, how will you establish membership parameters? For example, who will set them: the CoP's leaders or the CoP as a whole? How will you communicate the parameters to the group members? What will your new-member-orientation practices look like?

CHAPTER 3

# BUILDING THE FRAMEWORK

### Case Study: Resolving Concerns through a CoP

Simon, an early childhood special-education teacher, provides all his services outside the classroom to specific children with Individualized Education Programs (IEPs). But last month, Simon's supervisor informed him that at the beginning of the next school year, he (Simon) will switch to serving these children within an inclusive classroom. Simon is struggling to determine how to implement this directive in a way that will benefit all the children in that classroom. He fears that under this new arrangement, the children on his caseload will not get the services they need.

At the next meeting of the CoP to which he belongs, Simon shares this problem with his fellow members. Many of them are also special-education teachers and explain that they have struggled with the same concerns. However, they have found that the children on their caseloads actually show more growth in inclusive settings than outside of them. Intrigued, Simon continues to attend CoP meetings to learn more. He and his fellow members share the challenges they face and solutions that have and have not worked well. These exchanges give Simon a wealth of resources to use as he prepares to begin providing services in the classroom.

The framework for an effective CoP consists of the three components mentioned in chapter 2: a shared interest, a shared practice, and a community. The previous chapter discussed establishing a shared interest and laying the foundation of the community. This chapter explores the concept of community in more detail and explains the characteristics of shared practice. Understanding these concepts will help you establish key features that your CoP needs to thrive.

## Practice

The practice is a skill or set of skills that the CoP participants want to learn or strengthen. Some broad categories of practices include the ways in which professionals teach young children, interact with one another and with families, and administer programs. The following documents contain two of the most common sets of practices used in early childhood.

| Document | URL | Publisher | Sample Practices |
|---|---|---|---|
| ***DEC Recommended Practices in Early Intervention/Early Childhood Special Education 2014* (DEC Recommended Practices)** | https://divisionearlychildhood.egnyte.com/dl/tgv6GUXhVo | Division for Early Childhood of the Council for Exceptional Children | • "Practitioners promote the child's social development by encouraging the child to initiate or sustain positive interactions with other children and adults during routines and activities through modeling, teaching, feedback, or other types of guided support. . . .<br>• "Practitioners use a variety of planned and timely strategies with the child and [the] family before, during, and after [a] transition to support successful adjustment and positive outcomes for both the child and [the] family." |
| ***Developmentally Appropriate Practice in Early Childhood Programs Serving Children from Birth through Age 8* (DAP)** | https://www.naeyc.org/sites/default/files/globally-shared/downloads/PDFs/resources/position-statements/PSDAP.pdf | NAEYC | • "Teachers present children with opportunities to make meaningful choices, especially in child-choice activity periods. They assist and guide children who are not yet able to enjoy and make good use of such periods. . . .<br>• "Methods of assessment are appropriate to the developmental status and experiences of young children, and they recognize individual variation in learners and allow children to demonstrate their competence in different ways." |

A CoP could explore any individual practice or set of practices in these nationally recognized resources, including those listed in the table. The shared practice might relate to a particular developmental area; for instance, promoting critical thinking in young children is part of the broader area of cognitive development. A CoP could also select a certain approach to providing services, such as the primary service provider approach (described by M'Lisa Shelden and Dathan Rush) or the Pyramid Model for Supporting Social-Emotional Competence in Infants and Young Children (described by Lise Fox and Mary Louise Hemmeter), as its shared practice. By working together, the community members build a shared repertoire of resources, experiences, ideas, tools, core collective knowledge, and ways of addressing recurring issues within their field. All of these concepts together define the shared practice of the group.

### Case Study: Components of a CoP's Practice

A group of early interventionists would like to implement the primary service provider approach to serving families, but they struggle with changing from the transdisciplinary model, which they have used for years, and ensuring fidelity to the new model. This core group starts a CoP to share ideas, generate solutions to promote staff buy-in, develop training resources, create staff evaluation tools, and develop resources for families to explain the new model and the outcomes it will have. According to the Edmonton Regional Learning Consortium, this CoP's practice includes the new approach to service delivery, the specific practices (that is, ways of doing things) it contains, and all the resources that result from the community's work together.

## Dimensions of Practice

In his book *Communities of Practice*, Etienne Wenger asserts that to understand how practice is shaped in a community and how practice shapes a community, we need to look at three dimensions:

- mutual engagement, or how members interact with each other to create shared meaning regarding issues, problems, or both
- joint enterprise, or how members engage and work together
- shared repertoire, which consists of "routines, words, tools, ways of doing things, stories, gestures, symbols, genres, actions, or concepts that the community has produced or adopted in the course of its existence and which have become part of its practice"

It takes time and sustained interaction among the group to establish these three dimensions, but they are critical to attend to from the beginning of a CoP's existence. Let's take a closer look at each one.

### Mutual Engagement

According to Wenger, *mutual engagement* happens when members of a CoP interact with one another regularly to work together, share information, define the characteristics of the practices they use, and learn from each other. Members discuss real-life experiences, situations, and issues. They problem solve together, provide varying viewpoints to expand understanding, and indirectly share implied knowledge with each other and the community as a whole. These relationships, which develop through trust and respect, weave members into a social entity and keep them committed to returning to the community for support and solutions. Through mutual engagement, members establish or expand their identities as professionals and create much-needed trusting connections that enable them to grow and develop over time in their professions.

### Case Study: Brittany's CoP Connections

Brittany, a preschool special-education teacher, belongs to a CoP with teachers in similar roles. The CoP's shared interest and practices relate to implementing a new curriculum for social-emotional development, and the members regularly share their challenges with and ideas for the implementation. Because Brittany has been able to help others while getting ideas and emotional support herself, she continues to attend the CoP meetings. They help her feel more connected to the profession of special education, especially because she is the only special-education teacher in her building. Additionally, she has connected with Fernanda, an experienced special-education teacher, who continues to support Brittany through CoP conversations, emails, and the occasional in-person coffee meeting, all of which give Brittany a consistent go-to person for immediate help and support.

#### Joint Enterprise

Wenger asserts that *joint enterprise* means how members engage and work together toward a common goal. When a community forms, its purpose is often to create an opportunity to accomplish something on an ongoing basis. Members have some kind of work in common, clearly see the larger purpose of that work, and want to collaborate with others who have the same kind of interest and want to learn similar skills.

### Case Study: Using Joint Enterprise to Create a Key Document

In real life, one ECTA Center learning community (the ECTA Center's term for a CoP) focused on measuring child outcomes as part of the process of creating Individualized Family Service Plans (IFSPs) and Individualized Education Programs (IEPs) for young children with special needs. The members recognized that many states had developed forms, guidance documents, processes, and other materials that showed how to do exactly what the members were trying to accomplish. However, most group members kept smatterings of these resources on their personal devices, making it difficult to retrieve certain documents or to even remember where they were or what they were for. The group decided to create a document that would not only identify all these key resources but provide examples of how to use them and offer guidance for including families and other providers (such as medical professionals) at each point in the IFSP- and IEP-writing processes.

Creating this document was a joint effort among the members of the learning community. Various members worked on each of these tasks:

- Gathering resources to be included
- Categorizing resources, such as by whether they applied to the IFSP-writing process, the IEP-writing process, or both
- Developing instructions for using each resource
- Writing guiding questions and prompts for users to try with families and other providers
- Editing the compilation
- Determining when the final document was ready for publication

Once they had finished the document, the group members shared it throughout the special-education field to create awareness of best practices and resources.

### Shared Repertoire

The most common product of a CoP is a *shared repertoire*. Group members create a shared repertoire by continually developing and maintaining a shared set of resources and materials, which often includes procedures, techniques, shortcuts, tools, forms, symbols, actions, concepts, stories, and behavior patterns. Each of these resources, according to Wenger, provides a language for communicating meaning for the community and the practices it explores. The process of building this shared repertoire often creates a deeper sense of community among members, especially those members involved in creating and maintaining the materials. Members who have a shared history with the CoP, both through building a shared repertoire of resources and by participating in other CoP activities, create a certain sense of identity and belonging that leads to cohesion, trust, and respect among themselves and often attracts new members. Trust and respect are necessary to promote sharing of real-life experiences and learning from each other.

In some cases, developing a shared repertoire is the purpose of a CoP. In others, this activity happens along the way as members share their own resources and ideas. The process of creating one resource often stimulates thinking about what other resources might help the community and the early childhood field.

### Case Study: A Shared Repertoire on Executive Functioning

The members of one real-life CoP, who all worked at the same early childhood center, shared an interest in executive functioning in young children. Each member added any resources she had on this topic to a shared drive, which the group kept at their center so that all the teachers could use it. Eventually, the members noticed that their "library" had relatively few materials about executive functioning in young children with disabilities, so the CoP devoted some time specifically to researching and vetting resources on that topic to add to the drive. Now, when new staff start at the program, CoP members give them access to the drive, teach them how to use the materials, and invite them to join the CoP if they would like to learn more about executive functioning in young children.

## The Three Dimensions in Action

The following example demonstrates how all three dimensions of practice—mutual engagement, joint enterprise, and shared repertoire—work together to create a useful CoP experience.

### Case Study: Rosa Learns How to Help Nathan

A group of teachers working for a child-care franchise have formed a CoP in which they meet regularly and bounce ideas off each other through discussing real-life classroom problems, challenges, and successes (mutual engagement). Through these consistent meetings and the active role the teachers play in bringing in problems and challenges from their classrooms, the group members bond deeply and build their confidence and creativity (joint enterprise).

Rosa, a toddler teacher, enjoys these meetings because they provide an opportunity to learn from others within her organization. During today's discussion, she mentions that she has been struggling with the behavior of her student Nathan. He constantly interrupts other children while they play, knocks down their block structures, takes books away from them, and talks so much during nap time that he prevents anyone from resting. Rosa has tried everything she can think of to change Nathan's behavior, but nothing seems to work.

As the discussion continues, Rosa learns that many of the CoP members experience similar struggles with certain children in their classrooms. Each person shares his challenges and what solutions have and have not worked well. This exchange of ideas allows the teachers to gain knowledge from each other about handling challenging behavior, and they create a short list of tips to post in each classroom (shared repertoire). By the end of the meeting, Rosa has a number of ideas to try in her classroom, and she plans to share her results at future CoP meetings.

If you are a facilitator, use the worksheet in appendix A to begin gathering your thoughts on how to build mutual engagement, joint enterprise, and a shared repertoire in your CoP.

## Community

The last critical component to the framework for an effective CoP is community. To have a successful CoP, you must create a supportive organization in which members can pursue their shared interest through joint activities, discussions, problem-solving opportunities, information sharing, and relationship building. The Edmonton Regional Learning Consortium comments that a strong community fosters interaction and encourages a willingness to share ideas, enabling collective learning. The community component is influenced by the types of members in the group, how well each type is engaged, the recruitment and retention of members, and each member's investment in the CoP's work.

### Elements of Community Infrastructure

The infrastructure of each CoP varies. Key elements of a community's infrastructure include size, leadership, facilitation, communication, platforms, other logistical support, and financial support. Each element affects the CoP's functioning, sense of community, and ability to generate continued interest. Even if you are not a facilitator, it is important to understand how CoPs are organized and the type of support and connections that they offer. This information can help you make ongoing decisions about whether to join or leave a CoP and about your level of participation in one, all based on your own needs. Let's examine each characteristic in more detail.

#### Size

Some communities are small and intimate, while others consist of hundreds of people. Very large communities are structured differently than small ones and are usually subdivided by geographic region or by subtopic to encourage all members to actively take part. Smaller CoPs may still cover large geographic areas or several programs, or their members may all come from a single organization or school.

You might ask, "How large should my CoP be?" There is no specific quota for or limit to the number of members. Some challenges, such as difficulties in generating conversation, can arise in groups of any size. A smaller community may have limited ideas to pull from, but larger groups offer fewer opportunities for individuals to share their ideas or to talk directly to one another. A small community may allow for deeper, more meaningful relationships to form among the members that may endure past the life of the CoP. On the other hand, large communities offer wider perspectives and more ideas for members to draw on. Communities whose members are geographically scattered may find it hard to meet in person, while groups whose members all come from the same area may suffer from a lack of outside perspectives. Everyone in a CoP should be aware of how size and geography affect interactions within the group. If distance or numbers become problematic, leaders or members may need to make changes to help the group function better.

#### Leadership

No matter its size, a community needs internal leadership to create it in the first place and then to maintain and sustain it. Communities typically last longer and succeed better when leaders come from among the group members rather than from outside. Leaders from outside the community often have difficulty imposing a structure on it and cannot expect the community to thrive unless they join the other members in exploring the shared practice or interest.

### Case Study: A Ready-Made Facilitator

Joanie works at a school that includes grades pre-K through three. A CoP has formed among the staff to explore a shared interest in school culture. Coincidentally, Joanie recently completed a master's degree in education and wrote her thesis on this same topic. Her coworkers feel that, in combination with her excellent leadership and organizational skills, Joanie has the background knowledge to bring excellent insights and information to their discussion, so they select her to serve as facilitator.

### Facilitation

To ensure that meetings stay on track and accomplish their goals, that all members have a chance to speak, and that other organizational details are managed, a CoP needs at least one facilitator. We examine this important role further in chapter 4.

### Communication, Platforms, and Other Logistical Support

Each CoP needs defined communication strategies, both within and outside of meetings. These decisions also involve choosing platforms for sharing information. For example, when and how will members hear about CoP meetings? What format will those meetings use? What kind of follow-up will there be afterwards? There are many possible ways to meet these needs; choose the methods and formats that work best for your group members. For instance, you could appoint a communications manager who texts everyone a reminder before each meeting and sends out the minutes in an email afterwards. Some communities use a monthly conference call to share ideas and discuss issues, while others use a quarterly face-to-face meeting to build camaraderie and trust. You could use an online storage system for sharing resources or create joint documents, web pages, or wikis.

Beyond communication and platforms, logistical support involves many activities that help the community run and keep in touch before, during, and after meetings. The following list includes some of these tasks:

- Securing a meeting space for face-to-face meetings
- Scheduling and facilitating the use of electronic platforms or conference-call lines for virtual meetings
- Creating opportunities for participants to facilitate discussions in which they have a particular interest or to participate in meetings by sharing their work or the challenges they have encountered
- Creating meeting agendas
- Taking notes or minutes during meetings
- Organizing materials and keeping everyone on topic in virtual workspaces

### Financial Support

Though CoPs often cost less than other types of professional development, they do still need financial support to function. Some common costs include compensation for facilitators, staff time to participate in meetings and fulfill other commitments to the community, meeting-space rental, and technology costs, such as fees for using conference-call lines and online workspaces.

## Creating Effective Infrastructure

The key to creating effective infrastructure for a community is to ensure that the infrastructure works for the members and the ways they have chosen to collaborate. Some communities use a more informal approach to their work, focusing on having members check in with each other and bring up topics as they arise. Some CoPs are peer led, with one or more members of the community providing information or leading discussions. Some CoPs rely primarily on member presentations and follow-up discussions; others focus on identifying a common problem and working together to solve it over time. Many CoPs use all these collaboration methods, selecting which ones to use according to the needs of the membership.

For your CoP to operate as desired, you need to set up each infrastructure characteristic in a way that enables the group to function well. (If you are a facilitator, see appendix B for a worksheet that can help you with this process.) The members of a virtual CoP will probably not continue to connect with one another if they do not have access to an effective or accessible online platform. If, for instance, the members of a CoP all come from a single program and already feel overwhelmed with their work duties, they likely will not want or be able to take time outside of their regular workdays to meet. Thus, the group may not stay intact unless administrators allow CoP gatherings during staff-meeting times. Therefore, before you get too far into the process of setting up a CoP, make specific plans for each infrastructure component and share your plans with those who can make decisions and allocate resources to assist the CoP, such as directors, principals, or other authorities from outside the group.

### Choosing a Meeting Format

Sharing a practice requires regular interaction among the members. Many communities of practice start among people who work at the same place or live nearby, but members of other CoPs are distributed over wide geographical areas. Communities can function locally or at a state, national, or even international level, as noted by Wenger-Trayner and Wenger-Trayner in "Introduction to Communities of Practice." Therefore, some CoPs meet virtually, some face to face, and some in a combination of virtual and in-person meetings. Each community must consider its unique circumstances when deciding upon meeting locations.

Some people assume that CoPs work better when they can meet in person rather than virtually. While some face-to-face contact helps members put faces with names and build personal relationships, many CoPs function well by meeting only virtually. As important as meeting location, if not more so, is members' availability to meet and the amount of time the core group can give to the community to maintain its energy. Virtual meetings may also be more cost-effective to implement; in-person meetings need a physical space to gather in (which may incur a rental fee) and require members to travel to that location, while virtual meetings can use existing conference-call lines or free or inexpensive online platforms. But regardless of exact meeting location or platform, the most effective communities reduce confusion by having consistent meeting spaces. They also quickly adapt to members' needs by using multiple methods of engagement, such as displaying visuals (for example, on a slide or via screen sharing), sending materials ahead of time so members can review them before a discussion, or using a chat feature to prompt additional conversation during calls. Etienne Wenger, Nancy White, and John Smith argue that, regardless of the platform used to connect, the following factors are key to successful meetings:

- An appropriate rhythm of meetings over time, with a frequency and schedule that fit the members' lives
- Community-meeting practices, such as having agendas and a facilitator
- Attention to the experience of the participants, such as using a protocol to ensure that everyone feels welcome
- Flexibility in the agenda that allows for spontaneous interaction and the raising of unplanned but important topics

### Scheduling Meetings

Once you decide where the CoP's meetings will take place, you should define a regular meeting schedule (for instance, the third Thursday of each month from 3 to 4 p.m.). It helps to schedule ahead, perhaps through a full calendar year, to get the dates and details on members' calendars early and to promote attendance and continuity among members. Sending calendar invitations through email can both ensure that meeting dates are on the members' calendars and serve as a system for getting RSVPs as members accept or decline the invitations.

The lengths and frequencies of meetings will also vary from community to community. Some groups that meet in person, particularly if travel is required, may opt to meet a few times a year (such as quarterly) for several hours to make the most of the time they have together. Other CoPs, particularly virtual ones, may meet monthly for anywhere from thirty to ninety minutes. When deciding how often to meet and for how long, base your choice on the members' preferences. Initially, you can opt for a schedule based on the core group's needs and preferences, but openly discuss and periodically revisit the schedule with the other members as the CoP grows. These discussions and adjustments ensure that the frequencies and lengths of meetings allow sufficient time to share issues and solve problems as a group.

### Setting Up Ways to Share Resources

As community members work together, they create and share concepts, materials, and resources. Your CoP needs a platform or method for sharing these resources. Discuss the options with your fellow members and decide what will work best for your group. For instance, someone could share a useful article by emailing it to all members, posting a link on the CoP's website, or both. Some CoPs establish wikis, file-sharing sites, or online folders to store documents and resources that the members create or share.

## Levels of Member Participation

An effective CoP allows members to choose how and when to be involved. Each member participates at her own level, depending on her availability and needs. Striving to have many active members is a good goal, but a CoP also needs to provide room for those who want to benefit from the group but cannot devote as much time to it. Without such people, the CoP misses out on potentially valuable contributions.

In "Levels of Participation," Wenger-Trayner and Wenger-Trayner point out that CoPs typically have members functioning at five levels of participation:

- Core group
- Active members
- Occasional members
- Peripheral members
- Transactional members

Often a CoP has some members at each level, though the distribution may be uneven. To create a community that supports all members, we need to understand each level and the needs of the people in it. As Blankenship and Ruona remind us, participation in a CoP is voluntary, and while you can encourage people to join in, Wenger-Trayner and Wenger-Trayner caution in "Introduction to Communities of Practice" that each individual will always choose whether to participate and will engage at a level that is meaningful for her.

### Core Group

For a CoP to succeed, it needs a core group of members that, according to Scaled Agile, Inc., functions as the "heart of the community." This group often consists of the facilitator or facilitators and key leaders of the CoP, such as the members who first showed interest in the topic and the group. These individuals guide the purpose and the learning agenda for the community and take the needed, purposeful steps to build a network of members.

The core group, according to the Edmonton Regional Learning Consortium, is often the body that ensures that the purposes of the CoP remain clear over time. This group also collects members' feedback, often through conversations or surveys about the ways in which the CoP is (or is not) meeting individuals' needs, and regularly reviews, considers, and uses the results to adjust the CoP's activities and approach.

The core group maintains a healthy community for all members. They ensure that everyone has opportunities to speak and to be heard and that everyone respects and supports one another. Scaled Agile, Inc., lists the following examples of ways in which the core group can foster a healthy community:

- Keep things informal and simple.
- Foster trust by modeling how to share openly and protect information shared by others.
- Maintain the flow of communication among members to promote shared awareness.
- Increase the shared knowledge among members by forwarding information, resources, and tools as they become available.

According to Scaled Agile, Inc., the core group also sets up a network among members, nurtures the group by welcoming new members before they attend their first CoP meeting, facilitates sharing between participants, and promotes the CoP to new individuals who may benefit from joining it. The facilitator often comes from the core group and may call on it for support with some of her responsibilities, including organizing meetings, sending out reminders about meetings, and taking notes and sharing them with the group. The facilitator, whom we discuss in more detail in chapter 4, is a critical member of the core group and leads its efforts to keep the CoP's development moving forward.

### Active Members

The next level of participation in a community, as outlined by Wenger-Trayner and Wenger-Trayner in "Levels of Participation," is the active members. These members are highly involved in each meeting by encouraging others to join the conversation, by sharing what they have learned, or both. They are also a CoP's greatest champions because they eagerly share how much the CoP has benefited them, which may attract new members or encourage less-engaged members to put more time into the community. Active members regularly bring their challenges, successes, and lessons learned to the community, and they actively participate in the discussions about other members' challenges. Active members might work with the core group to establish the agendas for meetings, take notes, share materials, and recruit new members. They can often be counted on to share their thoughts during meetings or to encourage discussion when other members feel less like talking. Of all the groups in a CoP, active members tend to be the most interested in any joint efforts to develop resources (such as checklists, tools, documents, or guidance) for the CoP members, and they willingly put in extra time outside of meetings to get things accomplished.

It can be easy to confuse the core group with active members. Essentially, the core group consists of the people who hold the CoP together by making sure that the group is doing what it set out to do. They do much of their work outside of regular meetings. The active members do much of their work during meetings. They tend to be the movers and shakers of the group and to have lots of ideas.

### Occasional Members

Occasional members participate in a CoP during discussions on specific topics of interest or when they have specific challenges or information to share with the group. These members generally make up the majority of the membership in any community, as Scaled Agile, Inc., points out. They may seem uninterested in the CoP's work, but they often keep a low profile while staying on top of activities. They check agendas in advance and read the notes of meetings they do not attend so they can know when topics of interest come up, and they may check in with the facilitator or other members periodically just to stay connected. Occasional members learn from other members at their own pace and discretion, so they still actively participate—just in different ways than active members do.

### Peripheral Members

Peripheral members engage in CoPs on a limited basis. They may be newcomers to the group or have a more casual interest in the topic and stay involved to gain an overall, big-picture understanding of it. Members who start at other levels of participation, even the core group, may transition to peripheral membership over time as their interests and availability change. These changes can reflect a shift in a member's connection to the topic, such as a change in job or personal responsibilities, or they might simply indicate that the person's other commitments are taking over the time that the CoP used to occupy. While these changes are not bad, they serve as a reminder to continually reassess core-group and overall-group membership to maintain the CoP's structure and continuity. At the same time, make sure that the CoP's communication and presence are set up so that peripheral members can feel connected to and supported by the community.

### Transactional Members

Transactional members, as Scaled Agile, Inc., explains, are the members least connected to the CoP. Sometimes called lurkers, they might come to meetings just to listen to the discussion and glean what they need for their own use. In other cases, they do not even attend meetings but do access resources from the CoP's workspaces or other platforms. At times, transactional members may really want to engage in the topic but cannot get support to actually use the practice in their program. For example, a teacher might want to use Conscious Discipline in her classroom, but her director either is not invested in this model or is actively promoting the use of a different one in the program. Transactional members may not have time to do more than just listen during meetings. "Lurking" allows them to stay on top of relevant topics and information and to apply what they learn to their professional contexts if and when opportunities arise.

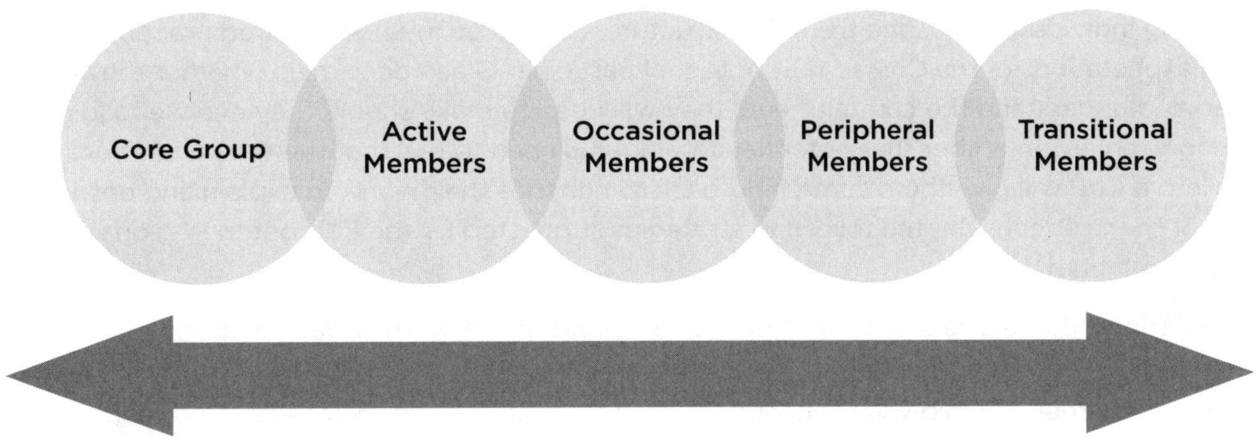


### Working with Members at All Levels

As stated before, the key to a successful CoP is creating space for each type of member and working to ensure that everyone participates in whatever way makes sense to her. Anyone can benefit at any level of participation, even the levels in which she does not engage as actively. The following list gives some benefits that members can gain at any level:

- Connecting with others in one's field or role
- Active contact with a broad network of practitioners in one's field
- Learning from other members
- Sharing passion for the work
- Feeling a sense of camaraderie ("These people get it. They know what it's like, and I don't have to explain why—just where, when, and how. Not only do they understand, but their questions support my passions, and their suggestions are helpful to my practice and to the

community as a whole.")

- Building a direct link between learning and performance—that is, easily taking information learned in the CoP and putting it directly into practice
- Creating trusting relationships

## Recruiting Members

Obviously, you cannot have a CoP without members. Finding interested individuals to participate in the community ensures multiple perspectives within the group. Recruitment efforts also help people become interested in and excited about joining and participating in the community. Therefore, you need to think through recruitment and "advertising" the community so that people are excited to give their time and energy to the group.

You can recruit CoP members in many ways. Both formal and informal invitations can work, depending on the potential purpose and vision of the group. Begin by identifying individuals who have questions or interests in common, and then suggest that they consider a CoP as a way to address those topics. If these people show interest in forming a small group, then you can invite them to help you start the CoP. Also consider extending a broader invitation to include those with alternate perspectives, those working in isolation, and those who may already have found some useful resources about the target topics.

When inviting individuals, describe the initial structure; the shared interests, shared practices, or both; and expectations of the CoP so that potential participants can determine whether they are interested and understand the commitments they will need to make should they choose to join. Just as importantly, remember that potential participants need to feel that the time and effort they put into a CoP will give them something back to enhance their work. To explain and ensure the value of the CoP, consider the following strategies suggested by the Edmonton Regional Learning Consortium:

- Choose topics that are relevant for all participants and based on their daily work.
- Describe how input from participants will make a difference in the group.
- Describe how membership will connect participants with others in their field of interest, including individuals they may not currently know.
- Offer resources.
- Generate excitement about collaborating to find new solutions.

As members begin to forge solid connections among themselves, the core group must create the environment needed for the community to begin collaborating successfully. These members play integral roles in organizing and launching the CoP and then in maintaining its energy and enthusiasm. They can market the CoP by sharing their vision with potential members. As the core group and other existing members demonstrate their willingness to invest in creating a network and sharing their knowledge and expertise, others will naturally be attracted to and more willing to invest in the community.

## Promoting Member Investment

One way to ensure that participants invest in the community is to articulate the short-term and long-term value of belonging to a CoP. Make it clear that members receive short-term value by getting expert help with immediate problems and spending less time searching for information, answers, and solutions. By using the expertise and perspectives of others, CoP members often come up with better solutions and make better decisions than they would on their own. In the long term, they develop a body of knowledge by solving routine problems, and they learn to document the best practices shared among the CoP members so that their collective knowledge can benefit future members and other early childhood professionals. It makes a difference when CoP members know that their efforts might help bolster their field by leading to improved professional practices, a new formalized body of knowledge, or policy or regulatory changes.

### Case Study: Origins of the Data Visualization Toolkit

In real life, the Center for Early Childhood IDEA Data Systems (DaSy's) CoP on data visualization produced so many ideas and suggestions from its members that it led to the creation of the DaSy Data Visualization Toolkit. This resource helps individuals in state and local early intervention and early childhood special-education programs present their data to various audiences for the purposes of making programmatic or policy decisions. This CoP created a new formalized body of knowledge for a segment of the early childhood field by identifying both a list of examples and the need to share the information outside of the CoP. Visit https://dasycenter.org/data-visualization-toolkit-2/ if you would like to explore this resource.

The CenterPoint Institute notes that CoPs can produce not only tangible results, such as a standards manual or other shared materials, but also less-tangible commodities, such as stronger bonds within the field, improved skills, or a renewed sense of inspiration or innovation. Indeed, many CoP members want to create tangible materials, and they and others outside the group will often judge the CoP's value by whether it produces such tools. But keep in mind that the intangible products of a CoP—including the feelings of professional confidence and identity that develop within members, the relationships they build, and the sense of belonging and spirit of inquiry that the group generates—are just as valuable as a handout or a report.

The results do not stop there. CoPs can help members become highly competent practitioners and move into leadership positions. CoPs can also inform practice and create change when needed in a practice or profession. Most importantly, CoPs create value by connecting the personal development and professional identities of practitioners to the CoP's shared interest, shared practices, or both.

Knowing all this, you must find ways to share it with potential CoP members. If they do not understand how they will benefit directly from participation, they will not invest the necessary time and effort, and the community will not thrive. Similarly, if principals, directors, and other decision makers across programs do not grasp the CoP's value to their individual organizations, they will not want to invest resources (such as their employees' time) to start or maintain the community.

## A CoP's Life Cycle

The lifespan of CoPs varies widely. Some exist over centuries, such as communities of artisans who pass their craft from generation to generation. Many CoPs last several years. Others—as noted both by Wenger, McDermott, and Snyder and by Dubé, Bourhis, and Jacob—exist long enough to accomplish a specific task or solve a particular issue. Many times, a CoP's lifespan depends on its objectives and the value it provides to its members.

CoPs are highly organic, meaning that they form without being forced and often without having a specific direction. Like most living organisms, they have a natural flow of life. This flow of life begins when potential members identify a shared issue, real-life problem, or situation and ends when the group members feel that they have achieved their objectives or that the group no longer provides value. In its article "Communities of Practice," Scaled Agile, Inc., declares that the core group must keep a pulse on this flow and periodically talk with the other members about the CoP's objectives or the value it adds to their lives. Ultimately, all members together decide whether the CoP should continue and in what capacity.

The following diagram, taken from the work of Wenger, McDermott, and Snyder, depicts the five typical stages in the life cycle of a CoP and lists the activities associated with each stage. During the CoP's creation, this diagram can help you identify where your CoP is in the cycle and what stage it may move into in the near future. This awareness can help you prepare ahead of time for the group's needs at each stage of the cycle.

| Potential | Coalescing | Active | Dispersed | Dissolution |
|---|---|---|---|---|
| People sharing similar situations without the benefit of a community | Members come together and recognize their potential for forming a group | Members engage in developing a community of practice | Members no longer engage very intensely, but the community still lives as a center of knowledge for the group | The community is no longer central, but people still remember it as a significant part of their identities |

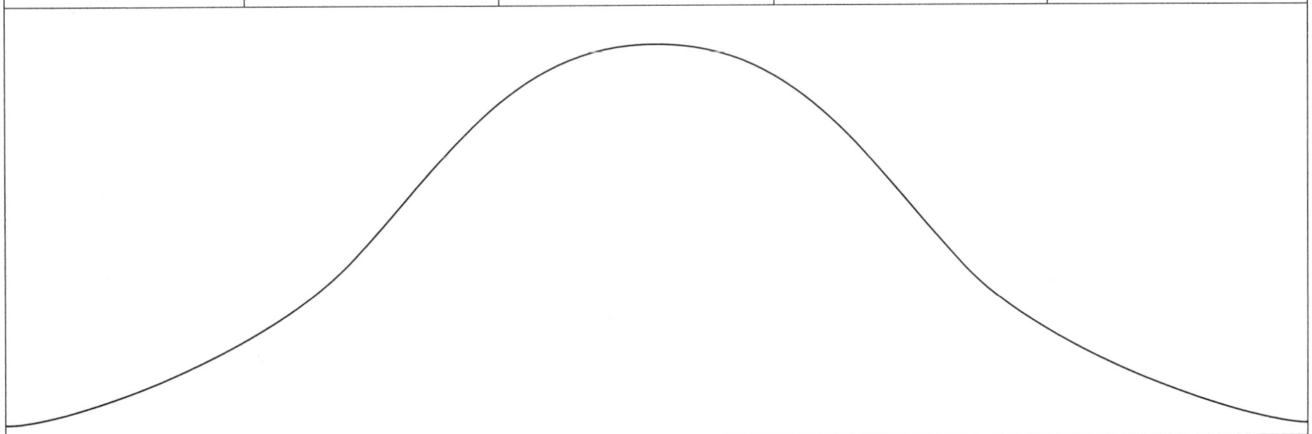

| Potential | Coalescing | Active | Dispersed | Dissolution |
|---|---|---|---|---|
| Finding each other, discovering commonalities | Exploring connectedness, defining joint enterprise, negotiating community | Engaging in joint activities; creating materials together; adapting to changing circumstances; renewing interest, commitment, and relationships | Staying in touch, communicating, calling for advice | Telling stories, preserving materials, collecting memorabilia |

**Source:** Adapted from Wenger, Etienne, Richard McDermott, and William Snyder. 2002. *Cultivating Communities of Practice: A Guide to Managing Knowledge*. Boston, MA: Harvard Business School Press. Used with permission.

## Potential Stage

As previously discussed, a community begins when people who share a common interest or passion decide to commit to learning from each other and sharing their experiences. This is the potential stage, when interested individuals begin to find each other and recognize their commonalities. These members often begin to form the core group for the community and help it move on to the next phase of growth.

## Coalescing Stage

During the *coalescing stage*, the CoP begins to take shape around the chosen issues or practices. At this stage, the core group establishes a structure that works for the current members. They decide on the frequency and format of meetings, how to share resources, who will facilitate, and how everyone will share information. They also set up membership parameters, which can be as restrictive or as broad as the core group chooses. All these guidelines help focus the purpose of the community and promote cohesion, trust, and respect among members.

### Active Stage

Once the CoP has an established shared practice and structure, the community moves into the active stage of engagement and learning. Members work together to solve issues, share experiences and materials, and create resources. Of all the stages in a CoP's life cycle, this one typically lasts the longest. It goes on as long as the community is useful and helpful to its members. Throughout the active stage, members continue building trust, finding support, and identifying commonalities, all of which build relationships and foster the growth of the community.

### Dispersed Stage

The community reaches the *dispersed stage* as members begin to participate and engage less in the group. This is inevitable and can happen for numerous reasons. As interests change, the members may no longer have a shared vision. Outside factors, such as competing commitments or changes to job responsibilities, may influence the level of investment that members are able or willing to make. Some members may have received the answers they were looking for or feel that they have gained all the knowledge they can from the CoP, so they no longer see benefit in sustaining it.

Regardless of the reasons, people will stop coming to meetings regularly. At this point, the remaining members will need to evaluate whether to continue the CoP. They have two options: they can dissolve the CoP or reestablish it with a new emphasis on a shared interest or practice that the still-active members can support. If the members choose to reestablish the CoP as a wholly different group, they may need to recruit new members who want to explore the new shared interests or practices. As long as members have an interest in improving their practices and maintaining the community, the CoP remains viable. However, if the CoP has accomplished its goals and the members do not want to switch to a new shared interest or practice, then it is time to dissolve the CoP.

### Dissolution Stage

The dissolution stage is the natural end of a CoP, and it is not something to be avoided. It may seem that the ending of a CoP signals some kind of failure, but it is quite the opposite. Instead, it means that the group has successfully accomplished its goals and its members are ready to move on.

At this point, the remaining members need to decide what will happen to the CoP's collective resources. This could mean storing materials virtually or keeping wikis or web pages accessible. You may also wish to hold a final meeting or send a last note to thank members for their engagement and participation.

## Chapter 3 Study Guide

What is the need for your CoP? In other words, what interests do you want to explore, or what practice do you want to improve?

Who has expressed interest in joining your CoP?

What outcome or outcomes do you hope to achieve through your CoP?

Based on the practice you will explore and the people who have expressed interest in learning about that practice, what types of activities would be most useful to your CoP members? Circle all applicable options, and list any other ideas you think of.

- **Innovation:** creating new ideas, new knowledge, and new practices
- **Improving practice:** sharing and supporting existing practices, guidelines, and strategies
- **Collaborative problem solving:** providing a forum for community members to help each other with challenges
- **Gaining collective knowledge:** organizing, managing, and stewarding a body of knowledge

Who might make good members of your core group?

Who might benefit the most by participating in your CoP, and who might best help you fulfill its purpose?

How many members do you want in the CoP? Should there be a target number for membership?

Is there anyone that the CoP would turn away if she wanted to join? If so, why?

How might involving new members enhance or conflict with the CoP's existing goals?

CHAPTER 4

# FACILITATION STRATEGIES

To keep a CoP stable and useful to its members, one of the most critical elements is skilled facilitation. Whether one person or several people facilitate, a CoP needs someone at the helm to handle a range of activities, from managing logistics to arranging content. A facilitator creates continuity for the community and ensures that it continues to meet members' needs over time. This chapter focuses on skills, behaviors, and strategies for effectively facilitating CoPs.

## Skills and Qualities of a Good Facilitator

What makes a good facilitator? Facilitation is not often expressly taught in formal education, so how do people learn to facilitate effectively? The research on facilitation—including work by the RI Board of Regents and by Wenger, McDermott, and Snyder—distills three characteristics that a facilitator must have to help his CoP succeed:

- Knowledge of adult learning and the CoP topic
- Organization
- Flexibility and responsiveness

A facilitator also needs a set of skills that can be difficult to define. Some might say that a good facilitator can listen well and follow a conversation as it evolves. Others might say that a good facilitator knows how to lead a conversation in a certain direction. While these skills are critical, a facilitator also needs other specific skills and personal qualities to effectively guide a CoP.

### Knowledge of Adult Learning and the CoP Topic

As the RI Board of Regents notes, a facilitator must understand how adults in general learn and how different types of adults learn. For example, some people think their ideas through as they talk, while others listen and then share their ideas. A good facilitator creates space for both types of individuals and ensures that the community provides opportunities for individuals to discuss and reflect on the information that they are trying to infuse into their practices.

Furthermore, a facilitator needs some knowledge of his CoP's focus area, including the overall shared interests and practices and the specific topics for each meeting. That is not to say that someone unfamiliar with the interests of the group cannot effectively lead a CoP; he can, especially because facilitators should also be good listeners who can aggregate individual and group feedback to help determine the course of the CoP. Wenger, McDermott, and Snyder argue that the facilitator does not have to be an expert; in fact, it is better when he is not. This may help keep the facilitator from dominating the conversation or from overly promoting a certain approach to a problem, two behaviors that interfere with the group's ability to pursue its own direction. However, in our experience, we (the authors) have noted that it helps considerably if the facilitator knows basic information about the topic, is well respected by his peers in the field, and is as passionate about the topic as the members are.

Interestingly, a facilitator with some background in the CoP's topic area becomes more effective in his facilitation duties. He can develop effective agendas and discussion prompts that allow the members of the community to have in-depth conversations during meetings. He makes better decisions about which members to ask to share their current work related to overall CoP interests or which external guests may have information that would benefit the group. As the facilitator follows members' conversations, whether in person or on electronic platforms (such as message boards), he better understands when the group is off track and how to either put it back on track or guide the members in a new direction. Critically, he can more accurately interpret the feedback that members give on their future direction, needs, or interests.

Having content knowledge enables the facilitator to participate in the community in more varied ways than he could without that knowledge, such as guiding the CoP in developing documents or resources related to the topic. For instance, one real-life CoP decided to produce a series of modules about early intervention, titled the Universal Online Part C EI Curriculum, under the leadership of a facilitator who had provided early intervention directly and had provided professional development to other early intervention providers. Because this facilitator was familiar with the content needed for the proposed modules, she could help develop the content outline, contribute content herself, guide the group's conversations, and support the members who led the project.

## Organization

The facilitator monitors and coordinates multiple aspects of community functioning. He keeps track of the details of the group, including the times and dates of meetings, and communicates those to members in a timely manner. This may mean planning meetings well ahead of time. For example, some communities establish their meeting times six months to a year in advance and send out information to the group to make sure that members set aside times for meetings and put them on their calendars.

Each CoP meeting also requires organization, including arranging for members or content experts to present at meetings and developing the rest of the agenda. To track the group's conversations over time and to make sure that absent members can stay up to date, the facilitator either takes notes himself or arranges for another member to do so at each meeting. In this way, the facilitator keeps detailed records of the CoP's conversations, activities, and decisions, and he makes that information available to each member in a timely way.

Finally, the facilitator tracks membership. He keeps contact lists current and updates the information when members join or leave the CoP. If a CoP has a website for members, he ensures that not only contact lists but also calendars, agendas, minutes, and materials are up to date, well organized, and easily accessible.

## Flexibility and Responsiveness

CoPs are designed to follow the interests of the group, so facilitators must be able to change direction, both on a small scale and a large scale. On a small scale, this can mean, for example, changing directions during a discussion but first checking in with the group, especially if the new topic strays significantly from the original content or purpose of the meeting. In this case, the facilitator might call for a pause and say, "I just want to check with the group—this discussion is very interesting, but I want to make sure that everyone's okay with this change of topic." The group can then decide whether to follow their current path or go back to the original topic.

On a large scale, the facilitator monitors members' interests over time and helps the entire CoP change direction and purpose when needed. This means that the facilitator must pay attention to the overall mood of the group and monitor participation. A healthy community has regular participation of a consistent set of members, while one that has dwindling attendance may need a change in direction or at least a check-in with its members. The facilitator must also gather information from the group over time to make sure that the community continues to meet members' needs. This information gathering may include informal conversations at meetings or formal assessments (see chapters 5 and 6) to gather information. The facilitator then makes adjustments based on the information that he receives.

Flexibility and responsiveness include allowing members to participate in the community in multiple ways and being responsive to each type of participant. For example, some members will naturally lead conversations, offer to share their work, and ask questions of others, while some members prefer to simply listen to conversations to glean what they can. A good facilitator ensures that meetings provide the opportunity for individuals to participate as they want, even if that form of participation changes at each meeting. Once the facilitator has a good handle on the different types of individuals in his group, he can plan the agenda, discussions, and activities to best match the group of participants at a given meeting. Flexibility over time will help the facilitator adjust as his group's makeup changes.

Lastly, flexibility and responsiveness include being respectful of the group's time. The facilitator makes sure that all meetings start and end on time and has a plan for each meeting so that the time spent meets the community's needs. Facilitators must also be dependable and responsible to their group. For example, a facilitator must plan out written communications, such as newsletters or email updates, and ensure that they go out to the membership when promised. If the community also has a website for members, he posts materials in a timely way and sends out meeting agendas and materials far enough in advance that members have sufficient time to read and review them before the meeting. The community decides what that time frame is, and the facilitator sticks to it.

## Healthy Discussion Skills

The RI Board of Regents explains that a good facilitator provides a model to his CoP's members, demonstrating the practices of inquiry, listening, and allowing everyone time to discuss freely without having to decide or act right away. When CoPs first start, members often want to solve all the world's problems! But a good facilitator places value on conversations, not just on solutions, and encourages others to think thoroughly about the issues at hand instead of rushing to conclusions.

Similarly, the RI Board of Regents notes that a skilled facilitator does not shy away from conflict. In fact, he can invite opposing viewpoints and even disagreements as a way of deepening the community's understanding of the topic. As long as the facilitator has created a trusting, mutually supportive environment, using conflict is a powerful strategy. For example, two teachers in a CoP may disagree about the best way to support effective transitions in the classroom, particularly for children with disabilities. Rather than debating the merits of each approach or trying to determine who has the "better" idea, a skilled facilitator will ask questions of each teacher to determine why each one believes that his technique works best. The facilitator might inquire, for instance, about the demographics of the children in each classroom (their ages, the ratio of boys to girls, what home languages the children speak, and so on), about any special needs among the children, or about the teachers' personal characteristics or beliefs that drive their decision making. Exposing these different perspectives helps the members of the CoP see why different approaches to transitions may work and how a teacher might adapt these approaches for different situations. It also models for the group how to talk about differences in practice without being concerned about judgement from others—in fact, it may demonstrate to others how to share their work and be open to the thoughts of others.

### Ability to Create a Safe CoP Environment

Creating a space where each member feels comfortable sharing, commenting, and asking for help is *the* challenge for every facilitator. So far, this chapter has discussed many of the factors that create this environment; another important factor is the CoP's organization. However, another key contributor is the dependability of the facilitator—responding to member inquiries in a timely way, sending out agendas and reminders ahead of meetings, and following up with notes and other next steps within a reasonable time frame all show the community that the facilitator is invested in the group. Lastly, a facilitator's ability to honor silence and processing time tells members that they have space to think before responding. Some facilitators struggle with this practice because they find it easier to fill silence than to let it be. If this is the case for you, try silently counting to ten before speaking. Most of the time, someone else will speak before you reach ten.

## Facilitator Responsibilities

Facilitating a CoP includes successfully managing multiple moving pieces over time. A facilitator's responsibilities break down into three categories: logistics and planning, meetings, and follow-up.

### Logistics and Planning

One of a facilitator's key responsibilities is to handle the logistics of the CoP. He must manage items such as meeting dates and times, the budget, communications, meeting spaces, and so on. (Appendices C and D contain useful checklists to help with these tasks.) Let's explore these items in more detail.

#### Dates and Times

Some CoPs meet at the same day and time each month, such as the first Monday at 2 p.m., while others opt to schedule the next meeting during the current one or by polls between meetings.

The facilitator should gather input from the CoP members to decide which approach works best. He may want to ask members to RSVP for each meeting so he can plan accordingly. For instance, if only four people plan to attend, the facilitator will probably not want to schedule an activity that requires groups of five.

### Canceling Meetings

To cancel or not to cancel? That is the question! Canceling a meeting should always be a last resort, as consistency is key when creating and sustaining a CoP. However, sometimes so few members can attend that you question whether the gathering will really benefit anyone. When this happens, consider polling the confirmed attendees and asking whether those people still want to meet or would prefer to cancel. Follow the participants' lead. If they still want to get together and talk, keep the meeting on the books. Sometimes great connections happen when only a few people gather.

### Meeting Space

*Meeting space* means different things for a group that meets in person than it does for a group that meets virtually. A face-to-face meeting will require a physical space that accommodates both the number of people in the group and the privacy needed for candid conversations. A virtual group needs technology to connect with one another. Often these groups use some combination of conference-call lines, webinar platforms, or video conferencing to connect. The facilitator must find out what technologies are available or obtainable with the CoP's existing budget. Options may include Adobe Connect, UberConference, Zoom, or GoToMeeting.

### Budget

Some CoPs have dedicated budgets that cover their costs, such as compensation for facilitators' time, fees to use meeting technology or an online platform, or rental payments for a meeting space. Often the facilitator develops and monitors this budget and uses it to pay for the needed items or services. In some cases, the facilitator may not have any responsibility for the budget because an administrator from the CoP's sponsoring organization monitors or manages these matters. Cost and budget should not be a hindrance to starting or maintaining a CoP; there are many free-to-use resources, including technology platforms, web pages, or conference-call lines, that can help CoP members connect.

### Communications and Membership Management

Perhaps most importantly, the facilitator handles communications and membership management. He takes care of communications with the whole group before, after, and between meetings (which we further discuss later in this chapter) and communicates with individual members as needed. He maintains a current list of members' phone numbers, emails, or both so members can access it. Facilitators should take every opportunity to encourage members to contact one another between meetings with questions or to discuss each other's work—this strengthens the community and ensures that those doing similar work can support each other and share information.

As new members join a CoP, the facilitator becomes their first and main contact. He welcomes them and makes sure they have access to all CoP information and begin to connect to other members. If the CoP uses new-member-orientation practices, the facilitator may complete them or delegate them to another CoP member.

The facilitator also acts as the CoP's historian. Wenger, McDermott, and Snyder explain that the facilitator has the important responsibility of keeping track of each meeting, including agendas and materials, so that members have access to past information. Many facilitators use secure websites to archive this information, which members with login credentials can access anytime. If members can also upload information for one another to these platforms, everyone has more opportunity to collaborate and communicate between meetings.

## Meetings

Meetings constitute the most substantial part of the work a facilitator does for his CoP. The tasks of arranging and facilitating a meeting can be divided into premeeting, during-meeting, and postmeeting tasks.

### Premeeting Tasks

#### Setting the Agenda

First, the facilitator plans the agenda for each meeting. This includes determining the topic or topics of conversation based on the topics of interest from the group, as determined by either an assessment (see chapters 5 and 6) or from interests shared in previous meetings. While the facilitator may have ideas about what the group needs to hear, he should keep his personal agenda and biases out of the planning. Doing so preserves the essence of the CoP as a group and honors the members' collective decision making about their own needs and direction. The facilitator decides how much time the group will spend on each portion of the agenda. Leaving adequate time for discussion and questions is critical, because the crux of a CoP is members' opportunity to share ideas and to ask one another questions. The agenda should also include time for a welcome, introductions (for everyone at the first few meetings and for new members at later meetings), and community updates, such as reminders or announcements about upcoming meetings, annual evaluations in which the CoP participates, or changes in schedule.

Once finished with the agenda, the facilitator can send it out to members ahead of time. A week in advance is a good time to do this. This practice reminds members about the meeting and helps prepare them for the upcoming discussion. It also motivates members to attend the meeting, as they can see how their input guided the agenda.

#### Preparing Presenters

If meetings include presentations or sharing of individuals' work, the facilitator plans these events in advance with those who will present or share. Based on the topic, facilitators identify individuals who have the expertise needed or have recent work, such as creating a new guidance document or successfully implementing a practice, in one of the CoP's areas of interest. Well ahead of time, the facilitator uses conversations, emails, or phone calls to invite these people to share their work.

When presenters agree to share their work at a meeting, the facilitator may want to offer to help them prepare. This can include informing presenters about the CoP members' interests and suggesting which aspects of the presenters' work to highlight or what resources to share with the group. The facilitator may want to offer presenters the opportunity to get feedback on their work from other members. If that sounds palatable, the facilitator may offer to help craft questions that will elicit the desired feedback while also promoting learning for the CoP members. He could review and comment on slides if there are not too many or could familiarize presenters with the CoP's technology, such as how to share screens or advance slides. For an in-person meeting, the facilitator may help presenters make sure they have enough copies of the materials they want to share. Finally, the facilitator should plan to arrive at the meeting early to make sure that the presenter is ready, all the technology is working, and the room is set up properly for the presentation.

At times, the facilitator may want to have plants, or people who will be ready to comment or ask questions if the discussion stalls, among the CoP members. This strategy works especially well for meetings that include presentations or general discussions among the members. As the facilitator gets to know the members, he can identify individuals who regularly participate verbally and are comfortable starting conversations but will not take over from the facilitator or a presenter. Then he can reach out to some potential plants before the applicable meeting, share the topic, and ask them to either respond to his questions or pose their own questions to the presenter. If someone else gets the conversation started, members who are more reluctant to share or ask questions will often feel more comfortable and join in.

### Arranging for Note Taking

The facilitator ensures that someone takes notes at each meeting. If a CoP has multiple facilitators, they may decide that one of them will take notes. In this case, it may help to designate one facilitator as the main note-taker but have both facilitators take notes and then combine them to form a more complete record of the meeting. A single facilitator may want to ask CoP members for assistance in taking notes.

#### Have a Plan B

In case a presenter cancels at the last minute, have a backup plan for the applicable meeting. You could, for example, call on a CoP member who is comfortable with last-minute requests and ask him to share a challenge or his latest work, or you might opt to share outside resources or your own work related to the day's topic and facilitate a discussion. The more familiar you get with the members of your community, the more options you have for Plan B.

### During-Meeting Tasks

As members arrive at or join a meeting, the facilitator welcomes each individual and does a bit of personal check-in, such as asking how the person is or how his day is going so far. The facilitator respects participants' time by making sure that the meeting starts on schedule.

During the meeting, the facilitator watches the time and helps the group stick to the agenda as much as possible. Simultaneously, as mentioned previously, the facilitator monitors the group's interest and follows the conversation where it goes, as long as members remain engaged.

The facilitator also pays attention to who speaks and whether the discussion is moving smoothly or stalling. If one or two individuals dominate the conversation, the facilitator can verbally invite others to chime or, if using an electronic platform for the meeting, can send this invitation through a chat function. If he has plants identified, he can call upon them to share or ask a question. Or he could switch to a new topic or comment on someone else's observation as a way to steer the conversation back to a fuller group experience. To prevent stalled discussions on a presentation day, the facilitator might prepare thought-provoking questions ahead of time. For instance, he could ask how members might use the presenter's information or whether they have encountered similar situations in their own work.

CoPs can avoid many during-meeting issues by discussing and establishing expectations with each other during their early gatherings. This way, all participants know that their time in the community will be respected, not wasted, and will assist their personal growth. Group norms might include allowing each person to finish sentences before beginning to speak, not interrupting, and asking questions in an inquiring, nonjudgmental way. CoPs may also opt to set norms for maintaining confidentiality, particularly when sharing works in progress or challenges that may involve people outside the group.

### Specific Tasks for Virtual Meetings

During a virtual meeting, the facilitator manages the technology smoothly so that technical issues do not bog down the members' experience. Some considerations include the following:

- **Background noise:** At the beginning of the meeting, the facilitator reminds individuals to mute themselves if significant noise occurs around them, such as from traffic or another conversation. If a participant seems unaware that, for example, his air conditioner is blowing loudly into his microphone, the facilitator can discreetly ask that person to mute himself and unmute when he wants to speak.
- **Chat responses:** The facilitator monitors what occurs in the chat and shares comments or answers questions verbally, as appropriate. This way, those who opt to share through chat can contribute in a meaningful way. The facilitator can encourage those who have commented in the chat to share more out loud if they would like to, but he takes care to not call anyone out. This behavior can put the person off, and it may make others worry that they may also be called out at any time. In any case, chat can be a helpful tool for those who may not be able to talk (for example, if they are in an airport or other loud place) or need some time to get comfortable with sharing aloud.
- **Screen share:** The facilitator makes sure that any presenters' materials are loaded and ready to share before the call. Remember, time is valuable! It is a waste of time for the members to watch someone search for and open a file. If the facilitator decides to share something on the spur of the moment, he turns off screen share until he has the item loaded. This practice provides a more coordinated flow to the meeting by making it easier for the discussion to continue until the item is ready.
- **Avoid talking through technology issues:** When something does go wrong with technology, which will inevitably happen at some point, the facilitator tries not to narrate his efforts to fix it. He knows that saying things such as, "I don't know why the screen won't share. I've clicked that button and, um—wait, let me see if this will work. No, that didn't work either. . . ." can turn

members off and make them lose patience with the process. Silence is okay, and it is okay to say, "Give me a moment, folks, to do some troubleshooting." Wenger, McDermott, and Snyder suggest designating a CoP member as a tech steward—in other words, someone who manages technology issues while the facilitator continues to run the meeting. This practice allows the facilitator to stop worrying about technical difficulties and continue the meeting while someone else fixes the technology.

#### Specific Tasks for In-Person Meetings

- **Side conversations:** The facilitator keeps an eye out for individuals having side conversations, which distract them and potentially the people around them. It may help if the CoP establishes early on how to manage side conversations. Even better, the group can devise a system in which they remind each other (rather than the facilitator giving all the reminders) to minimize or eliminate these conversations.
- **Technology use:** At the beginning of the meeting, the facilitator asks CoP members to turn off cell phones and tablets and place them facedown to avoid repeated distractions from notifications. He also asks that people use laptops only for meeting purposes and not answer emails during meetings.

### Postmeeting Tasks

After each meeting, the facilitator completes a handful of activities to close the loop on that meeting before starting the planning for the next one. One important reason for these activities is to make sure that the CoP members have access to the resources from the meeting. This is especially important for members who could not attend; having quick access to the information enables them to keep up with the conversation as their time allows.

#### Sending Follow-Up Communications

After each meeting, the facilitator completes these communication-related tasks:

- **Thank the presenter:** The facilitator uses a quick message, email, or call to thank the presenter for his efforts to share and his willingness to participate in the CoP in this way.
- **Compile the notes:** The facilitator gathers the notes from those who took them and makes sure that they are understandable and free of misspellings and other distracting errors. If the CoP has letterhead or a logo, he includes it on the notes.
- **Post the agenda, resources, and notes:** The facilitator uploads the notes and all other materials from the meeting to the CoP's platform, such as a wiki or secure site. This may include information from the presenter as well as any resources that were discussed during the meeting.
- **Send a follow up email to all members:** In this email, the facilitator includes another thank-you to the presenter, attaches copies of the notes and other materials, and includes a link to these resources on the CoP's platform. Though it may seem redundant to both post the materials on the site and send them in an email, using both methods increases the likelihood that members will be able to access the resources. For instance, even if a member has technical difficulties downloading a handout from the website, the email attachment might work for him.

- **Action steps:** The facilitator identifies any actions that seem to emerge from the CoP over time. Sometimes the community may identify a shared need that requires members to work together between calls, perhaps on a document or a resource that will help the members implement a new practice in their own work. The facilitator keeps track of these needs, such as by maintaining a list on a Google document, and, during a meeting or a series of meetings, works with the CoP members to identify ways to address each need.

### Promoting Connections

The facilitator promotes teamwork and collaboration across the CoP. At times, members may identify the need to talk with each other more about their work outside of CoP meetings. If needed, the facilitator may offer to support these connections by emailing those interested, setting up a call, and participating in the initial discussion.

Facilitators may also find ways to connect themselves to members between meetings. Wenger, McDermott, and Snyder call this "walking the halls," which means that the facilitator reaches out to members between meetings with questions, prompts, reflections, and resources, all based on in-meeting conversations. It requires that a facilitator be an excellent listener to individual comments and requests for information and then follow up with each person to find out whether other CoP members have met that need and to share any resources that might help. Reaching out in this way helps members connect with the facilitator and begins to create trusting relationships between individuals.

### Sharing Resources

Between meetings, the facilitator might find additional resources on the group's topic of interest. Via an email, a post on the community's site, or both, he can share this information with the group members for their consideration.

### Monitoring Discussion Boards

Many communities continue discussions or start new ones between meetings via discussion boards. The facilitator monitors these, answers questions as appropriate, and provides resources and additional questions for consideration. To keep the collaborative team approach intact during these virtual interactions, the CoP sets expectations early on that the discussions will take into account each member's perspectives and ideas and that all participants will be respectful to each other.

## Collaboratively Developing Tools and Resources

Sometimes CoP members opt to bring their expertise and experience together to create a new resource or tool for themselves, to share with other professionals, or both. The facilitator's role in this work may vary, but unless the entire CoP is working on the same resource, he ideally plays a support role only. When smaller groups of members are working together, the facilitator may opt to provide mostly logistical support, such as creating calendar invitations, taking notes, or making copies, so that members can take on more of the facilitation role with the joint work. The facilitator must be prepared to be flexible and allow his role to change over time based on the needs of the group producing the new work. Even when a project is a full-CoP effort, another member (such as one who has specialized knowledge of the applicable topic) may be better suited than the facilitator to lead the joint work.

If the facilitator temporarily takes a support-only role, either with the full group or with a smaller working group, he ensures that that group acts as a team: respecting and using each person's expertise, listening to each other's opinions, and sharing responsibility. He can promote collaboration in the group by helping them develop an action plan. This plan should include a vision for the joint work, deadlines and parameters to prevent mission creep, and key roles and responsibilities. In this way, each member knows what he will contribute to the joint work, and the facilitator does not end up doing all the work instead.

## Facilitating through the Life Cycle of a CoP

Beyond managing meetings and ensuring individuals' meaningful participation, a facilitator has some extra responsibilities at certain points in a CoP's life cycle. These factors affect how he needs to carry out typical activities and use his facilitation skills.

### Potential Stage

During the potential stage, when a CoP is just being established, the facilitator takes a strong hand in generating energy and excitement about the enterprise. In a way, he is the initial champion of the group. He often has a strong interest in the CoP's topic, so his enthusiasm can spur others to get together and create the group. When he has great ideas for the conversations that occur about the shared interest or practice, he begins reaching out to other members and asking for their insights and ideas.

At this point, the facilitator spends most of his time learning more about the initial participants' needs and creating group structures and plans accordingly. He tries out different communication strategies and meeting platforms and gathers continuous information from the members until the community begins to settle down and work well for the members. He also watches for individuals who show potential for and interest in leadership, and he begins to nurture those people in preparation for them to eventually take on leadership roles.

### Coalescing Stage

During the coalescing stage, the facilitator assesses the effectiveness of the CoP's methods, including how the members gather for meetings and their ways of storing and sharing documents and communicating. He takes note of patterns in attendance at meetings and may follow up with individuals whose attendance has dropped, trying to find out whether changes in the CoP might help or whether these individuals simply have scheduling conflicts. Facilitators also seek ongoing feedback from the entire group to determine what adjustments are needed (see chapters 5 and 6). Individual emails or calls to members or a simple *plus-delta* at the end of each meeting may help.

### What Is a Plus-Delta?

A plus-delta is an easy way to find out what is going well (plus) and what needs to change (delta) in a CoP. A facilitator can leave about five minutes at the end of each meeting to ask the simple questions "What worked well in today's meeting?" and "What can we improve for next time?" He may want to track participants' answers over time as part of a continuous quality-improvement process.

The following table presents some sample plus-delta questions.

| Plus | Delta |
|---|---|
| • What went well in this meeting?<br>• What did you like about the topic or format of the meeting?<br>• What would you like to explore further? | • What did not go well in the meeting?<br>• What suggestions do you have to improve future meetings?<br>• What would you like to explore further? |

## Active Stage

During the active stage, the facilitator mostly focuses on maintenance and keeping things up to date. As a CoP becomes more established, the members may opt to begin some work together to produce a new tool or resource, so the facilitator helps the group navigate the planning, implementation, and sharing of this work. Once a CoP is well established, the facilitator uses more-formal methods of evaluation not only to gather data on individual members' needs but also to learn more about the impact the CoP is having on individuals' work and professional growth.

Within an established CoP, a facilitator may sometimes note that transitions are needed. Perhaps members have lost interest in the original purpose of the community and begun focusing on different topics in their discussions. Perhaps a cofacilitator unexpectedly takes a job in a different field and leaves the CoP. A facilitator must be familiar enough with the CoP to understand how these types of changes will affect it. He also needs to know how to bring these topics up with the members to get suggestions and make the needed changes.

Note that a change in facilitators is not bad. While individuals may join a group because they feel drawn to both the topic and the facilitator, a change in leadership can bring a much-needed breath of fresh air, offering different approaches and perspectives on the topic of interest. A leadership change has a particularly strong effect when a regular CoP member asks to step into a facilitation role with the community. Ideally, the existing facilitator has already been mentoring this person for some time, providing important preparation for this transition.

## Dispersed and Dissolution Stages

Two separate studies—one by Dubé, Bourhis, and Jacob and another by Wenger, McDermott, and Snyder—conclude that in some classic, business-oriented definitions, CoPs are often time-limited and focus on a single problem to solve. However, in the early childhood field, a CoP may have a long life span because the group can take different approaches on the same topic or shift topics altogether. Still, sometimes it becomes clear that a CoP has run its course. Participation may decline steadily. Even the most regular participants might stop attending meetings. The same topics may continually resurface in small-group conversations. Any of these reasons might signal that the CoP's life cycle is winding down and that the participants should consider disbanding.

At this point, the facilitator assesses need and determines whether there is still sufficient interest to continue the CoP. While he should gather input from the members, he also needs the power to ultimately decide what makes the most sense. There will almost always be a few people who want to continue the CoP even when others are clearly no longer invested. In this case, the facilitator can offer other options for working together, such as continuing conversations via email or a discussion board, sharing resources, or even holding an ad hoc meeting when new information or challenges arise. The dispersing CoP could even merge with another CoP that discusses similar topics, if one is available and both sides agree.

On the other hand, the CoP members or the facilitator may consider all the alternatives and still choose to dissolve the group. After this decision, the facilitator completes the following tasks:

- **Ensure continued access to archived information:** The facilitator makes plans to either close out or continue the maintenance of any electronic storage of CoP documents. If no one can keep the storage available long term, he makes copies of all documents, such as by putting them on a thumb drive or other external storage, and gives CoP members the opportunity to download what they want a few weeks prior to the closure date. If the electronic storage will remain open, the facilitator arranges with interested individuals to keep their access open.
- **Host a final meeting:** If the remaining members are interested, the facilitator may lead one last meeting of the group. This can be an abbreviated version of the usual meetings and can include sharing resources, discussing next steps, and making plans for future work.
- **Send final notes and contact information:** Following the final meeting, if there is one, the facilitator sends all CoP members the last set of notes, including (with everyone's permission) contact information for all members. He encourages everyone to reach out to one another if questions or challenges related to the topic of interest arise.

## Supporting Member Involvement at Each Stage

Throughout the life cycle of the community, the facilitator will find that he has different types of participants to interact with and support. To recap, Wenger, McDermott, and Snyder define each group as follows:

- **Active participants:** individuals who regularly attend meetings and speak up to share information and ask questions
- **Potential leaders:** individuals who could become leaders within the community by cofacilitating or leading product or tool development

- **Lurkers:** individuals who sometimes come to meetings and often only listen

Regardless of the types of participants or the number of each in his CoP, the facilitator supports each type's participation and involvement. Taking caution, for example, to avoid spontaneously calling on a less-verbal attendee will ensure that that person feels comfortable coming to meetings and participating in a way that is meaningful for him. Similarly, looking for opportunities for those who would like to share leadership will ensure that the community experience is meaningful for them as well, though in a different way than for someone who just wants to listen.

### Case Study: Two Levels of Participation

Linda and Dina both enjoy participating in a CoP about IFSP development. In a recent call, the group decided to develop an easy checklist to help practitioners ensure that they use family-centered practices when creating IFSPs. Linda offered to lead this effort for the group, so she has become the coordinator for the small group of members who want to help develop the checklist. Dina, on the other hand, decides to simply attend the calls in which the checklist will be on the agenda and to track when it will be finished so she can consider using it.

## Team Facilitation

Facilitating a CoP is a lot of work, but it does not have to be a solo job. In fact, it adds an element of quality to have a team facilitate the community. When more than one person facilitates, the CoP will more likely benefit from all the characteristics of a good facilitator. A pair of facilitators, each with his own strengths in facilitation, can complement one another's skills and abilities and offer the community a more stable foundation of facilitation. It also provides an excellent opportunity for the facilitators to model effective teamwork and collaboration practices to the CoP members. While there currently is no research to suggest the optimal number of facilitators for a group, conventional wisdom suggests carefully considering whether there should be more than two or three. When too many individuals try to make key decisions or coordinate multiple aspects of the CoP, confusion and lack of unity may result. In the authors' experience, it works well to have two to three individuals who collaborate and share the load of managing the CoP.

There are several ways that a team of facilitators can build a strong foundation of teamwork.

First, each facilitator can have a separate role based on either his strengths or content expertise. For example, Martinique is very organized and takes superb notes, so she keeps track of the details of membership, agendas, and speakers and takes minutes at meetings. Xiu, on the other hand, listens well to conversations and accurately synthesizes information, so she acts as discussion leader during meetings. In this case, the facilitators take on the responsibilities that best suit their skills, and they complement one another's abilities so that their CoP members benefit from all the characteristics of a good facilitator.

In other cases, facilitators may have different content knowledge that complements various interests that a group has. Each facilitator takes primary responsibility for CoP activities that relate to his area of expertise. For example, a CoP that focuses on developing social-emotional skills in young children may be cofacilitated by Frank, a classroom teacher of four-year-olds, and Aliyah, a child-mental-health specialist who is an expert in social-emotional development. This combination ensures that the participants get the expertise they need for each topic.

There are many ways that facilitators can take turns (tag-team) leading meetings and managing the overall organization of the CoP. For example, each facilitator might lead different portions of a discussion during a single meeting; they can plan this switching off in advance or tag-team spontaneously based on the turn of the conversation. If a CoP meets monthly, one facilitator might manage all CoP logistics, communication, and facilitation for one month, and then the other facilitator could handle these matters until the next meeting.

Facilitators can also share responsibilities by covering for one another when one person has to miss meetings because of other responsibilities, vacation, or illness. When all facilitators equally share tasks for each piece of the CoP, one individual can easily step away and the community can continue uninterrupted. Facilitators also become less fatigued because they share the load of the CoP.

Cofacilitating works best when the facilitators trust and respect each other and when they understand how each facilitator contributes his own strengths to the CoP. If the facilitators have worked with each other in other capacities, such as if they are coworkers, they may have already done some of this work. If they have not yet worked together, they may want to spend some time talking about their strengths, preferences, and expectations for how the partnership will work. Whether experienced or new partners, facilitators should set clear expectations with one another about how they will manage each other's time off and who will handle which responsibilities before, during, and after meetings.

Facilitators particularly need to talk about how to manage each other's "off" days. Everyone has days when he does not function at his best—for example, when he does not feel physically well, has had a difficult day, has personal issues pressing on his mind, or a combination of the three. Facilitators need to be able to tell each other when those days happen, and they need to decide how they will manage these days. While it is not ideal, one facilitator may need to go solo on such a day so his colleague can attend to the outside issues. Alternatively, one facilitator may need to take the lead for the day while the other takes on a lesser role, one that matches the energy and attention he can give.

## Chapter 4 Study Guide

Based on the descriptions of an effective facilitator in this chapter, what are your strengths as a facilitator?

What are your weaknesses as a facilitator?

How comfortable are you with conflict? with silence?

What can do you do to improve your comfort with conflict, silence, or both to help you facilitate a CoP effectively?

Who might make a good cofacilitator for your CoP?

What characteristics does this person have that will complement yours?

______________________________________________

______________________________________________

______________________________________________

______________________________________________

How might you split the responsibilities of facilitation with this person?

______________________________________________

______________________________________________

______________________________________________

______________________________________________

As cofacilitators, how will you promote connection and resource sharing among members outside of meetings?

______________________________________________

______________________________________________

______________________________________________

______________________________________________

CHAPTER 5

# ASSESSING A COMMUNITY OF PRACTICE

## Case Study: Carrie Learns about Assessment

Carrie has facilitated a CoP for the past eight months. When she first started, she completed an assessment to guide her facilitation and planning for the CoP and to ensure that the CoP met its members' needs. Initially, members engaged in lively discussion on regular video calls. Recently, however, many members have stopped coming to calls, and those who come do not say much. Carrie does not know what to do. She shares her concerns with Chantel, a colleague who facilitates another CoP.

**Chantel:** Have you assessed the needs and interests of your CoP members recently?

**Carrie:** Well, I've been using our discussions to informally assess what the members are interested in. But I haven't done anything beyond that—I wasn't sure if I needed to.

**Chantel:** Informal assessment is important; it helps you keep track of the members' interests over time. But if people aren't engaged, it may be time to do something more formal to figure out what's going on.

**Carrie:** Like what?

After discussing some ideas with Chantel, Carrie sends an electronic survey to her CoP members to gather information about what is affecting their level of engagement. When the members respond and Carrie evaluates the data, she finds two main trends. First, many people have scheduling conflicts with the regular meetings. Second, Carrie has been letting the conversation go where it will in meetings, but the CoP members strongly prefer having planned discussion topics so that they know they will get something valuable from attending.

Based on these results, Carrie switches the regular meetings to a more convenient time and begins sending out a formal agenda for each meeting in advance. She also starts to collect feedback from CoP members more regularly and uses it to plan future meetings on topics of interest to the members. The CoP begins to thrive once again, and membership nearly doubles within a year. None of this would have happened if Carrie had not assessed the CoP and acted to meet the needs she discovered.

Like Carrie, you may have started your CoP and now see it running smoothly. All may appear well. But how can you know for sure? Just as early childhood professionals regularly assess the children in their care and evaluate the results, you need to regularly assess your CoP and evaluate the results to make sure that the CoP achieves its purpose and meets members' needs. Without these regular checkups, as Carrie's experience shows, you can miss important signals about how to keep the CoP relevant and useful to its members.

So where do you start? How do you effectively assess and evaluate something as complex as a CoP? The terms *assessment*, *evaluation*, and *data* may even sound a bit intimidating. However, you already collect and evaluate data in many ways to make choices. For example, when you weigh yourself on a scale or when you check your speedometer to see if you need to slow down or speed up, you gather data and make decisions based on it. This chapter will help you start to do the same thing with your CoP.

If you are not a facilitator, you may think, "But I'm not in charge. Why do I need to worry about assessment?" Whether you facilitate or simply participate in your CoP, you play an important role in determining its success, and an important way to do that is to participate in assessment. As a facilitator, you will likely spearhead assessment efforts. As a CoP member, you will provide information and input as requested about your experiences with the CoP and how it has affected your practices as an individual. Reflect on your role as you read this chapter, and identify ways that you can contribute to assessment activities.

## Why Assess Your CoP?

To understand the need to assess CoPs, we must first define the terms *assessment* and *evaluation*. Though these words are often used interchangeably, they refer to different procedures that have distinct purposes. In this book, *assessment* is the ongoing process of gathering information (data). This can be done formally (such as through a survey) or informally (such as by reflecting on members' engagement during a meeting and on the feedback they provided while there).

The data are then used to monitor progress and make decisions—this is *evaluation*. This chapter focuses on assessment (collecting data), while chapter 6 focuses on evaluation (using the collected data).

The facilitator typically takes charge of assessment efforts because she needs to consistently collect data to make informed decisions for the CoP. By gathering this information, the facilitator and the members can begin to understand the members' changing needs, what works well, what needs improvement, and what impact the CoP has on individuals and their organizations. In other words, assessment is part of the regular maintenance for a CoP. If a CoP starts to falter, assessment becomes even more important, because it will help the facilitator and members discover how to get the CoP back on track.

## Creating Assessments

There is no standardized assessment for CoPs. Each facilitator creates assessments for her CoP based on its unique characteristics and circumstances and what information she needs to gather.

While this may sound overwhelming, it need not be. The process of creating any assessment has four steps:

1. Determine your purpose.
2. Determine what type of data you need.
3. Determine how to gather the data.
4. Determine when to assess.

Let's look at each step in more detail.

## Determine Your Purpose

Before making any other decision about an assessment, you need to understand its purpose. In other words, you first need to establish what you need to know at the end of the assessment and why you need to know it. The facilitator usually determines the purpose of any proposed assessment. However, if the CoP is supported or financed by an organization, then the organization may provide input on the purpose.

The following table lists some situations that might warrant conducting an assessment and what its purpose might be.

| Situation | Possible Purpose(s) of Assessment |
|---|---|
| Meeting attendance is down or fluctuating. | To discover why this is happening so that we can **get more people to consistently attend** |
| New interests are emerging among members. | To determine whether the CoP should shift its overall focus to align with these new interests so that we can **continue to meet members' needs**<br><br>To determine whether members should form a subgroup so that **they can pursue their interest without detracting from the overall shared interest and practices** |
| Stakeholders are benefiting from the CoP. | To identify what about this CoP is so effective so that **we can continue doing whatever it is** |

Purpose directly affects all other elements of an assessment, including the following:

- What types of data you need (qualitative or quantitative) and therefore what types of questions you ask
- Whether you use formal methods (such as questionnaires) or informal ones (such as discussions) to collect the information
- When, including how frequently, you complete the assessment
- Who completes the assessment (everyone or only certain CoP members)

As we explore the rest of the steps in the process of creating an assessment, we will explore these factors as well.

## Determine What Type of Data You Need

Assessments produce a wide range of data that falls into two main categories: qualitative and quantitative. The type of data you receive from an assessment depends on the questions you ask in that assessment. Each type of data provides different but equally important information and is useful for different purposes.

### Qualitative Data

Qualitative data is descriptive and open-ended. Questions that produce this type of data are called qualitative questions. When responding to qualitative questions, participants can explain their answers and share their opinions and experiences. This provides specific, detailed information. However, when you collect large amounts of qualitative data, it can take a long time to analyze all the responses and use the results objectively to make informed decisions. This happens because, according to Blankenship and Ruona, qualitative data analysis requires that we be able to look at the data to determine important meanings and patterns in the information.

#### Sample Qualitative Questions

- What is one thing you learned from today's discussion?
- What is one thing you plan to try or apply as a result of your participation in today's meeting?
- What other topics, resources, or supports are you seeking from the CoP?
- Other comments, questions, or suggestions you would like to offer: ______________

______________________________________________

### Quantitative Data

*Quantitative data* is easy to measure and analyze. Questions that produce this type of data are called *quantitative questions*. Though the term *quantitative* may suggest statistics, scores, and other information expressed in numbers, these are not the only kinds of quantitative data. Any question that forces respondents to choose from a limited number of answers—such as yes-no, true-false, multiple-choice, rating-scale, or ranking questions—produces quantitative data.

### Case Study: A Simple Quantitative Question

In a CoP that explores ways to help children with special needs, Harriet sends this quantitative question to members between meetings:

> Rank these possible topics for our next discussion according to your priorities. Put a 1 by your first choice, a 2 by your second choice, and a 3 by your third choice.
>
> ___ How do I deal with challenging behaviors in children with special needs?
>
> ___ How can I help a child who appears to have special needs but does not officially have a diagnosis?
>
> ___ A child in my care just received an IFSP—now what do I do?

When the members respond, Harriet can quickly determine the group's overall preference by adding up how many points each option received. The lower the total for a particular answer (remember, a ranking of one represents a person's top choice), the greater the number of members who consider it a high priority.

Quantitative questions can be particularly useful, as Wenger, Trayner, and de Laat point out, because you can easily reuse them for multiple assessments. This technique saves time and enables you to compare and correlate data between questions or across time (trends), a valuable tool when you want to understand what effects a CoP has had on members and their practices.

However, quantitative data has one major drawback: it does not necessarily explain the reasoning behind responses. For instance, a survey item might ask the respondent to rate whether she strongly agrees, somewhat agrees, somewhat disagrees, or strongly disagrees with a given statement. If Zavier checks *disagree*, this response provides clear quantitative data. But without qualitative data, only Zavier knows why he answered as he did.

## Sample Qualitative Questions

What part of today's meeting did you value most? Circle your answer.

- Introductions
- Updates
- Sharing resources
- Sharing challenges or asking questions and getting help
- Discussion
- Other (please describe):

Did you identify at least one strategy to support you?

- Yes (please describe):

- No

Did you share a resource or strategy with others?

- Yes (please describe):

- No

In what ways did today's discussion help you? Select all that apply.

- I learned about new tools I can use.
- I found something new that I would like to try.
- I gained an idea that I would like to further develop.
- I developed relationships with people who can help me.
- I gained confidence in my skills, abilities, or both.
- Other (please describe):

You may notice that some of the sample quantitative questions also ask for qualitative data ("please describe"). These examples demonstrate how both types of data work together to give you a more complete picture of what CoP members think and need.

## Determine How to Gather the Data

Once you have established the purpose of an assessment and the type or types of data you need, you need to consider the best way to gather that data. You can use formal methods, informal methods, or a combination of the two.

### Formal Methods

The following table presents some formal methods of collecting data, including both potential tools and possible question types.

| Tools | Possible Types of Questions to Ask |
| --- | --- |
| • Premeeting registration form that collects demographic information and asks open-ended questions about requests and priorities for that meeting<br>• Apps or programs, such as Poll Everywhere, that allow members to anonymously respond to a question by text message or SMS (useful for in-person meetings)<br>• Polling, chat, or emoticon features in an online meeting room<br>• "Parking lot" that collects information using sticky notes, chart paper, or both<br>• Surveys or questionnaires<br>• Focus groups<br>• Interviews<br>• Knowledge tests<br>• Reviews of records, such as meeting-attendance logs<br>• Direct observation, such as watching videos of members in which they demonstrate changes in their practices | • Multiple-choice questions<br>• Rating-scale questions, such as asking how much a respondent agrees or disagrees with a statement<br>• Ranking questions, such as asking a respondent to mark her highest priority as 1, her second-highest priority as 2, and so on |

Because formal methods often use a written, organized format, such as a questionnaire, you can easily document and track responses. In turn, you can more easily analyze and organize this data and use it for multiple purposes, including evaluating the CoP over time. Formal methods frequently permit members to reflect before responding to prompts and to answer in private; both factors can lead to heartfelt answers. You can also collect demographic information, qualitative data, *and* quantitative data with a single assessment, which is harder to do with informal methods.

However, formal methods also have their downsides. To collect and store information, they need a tool or platform, which you might have to pay for. They also take planning and time to set up, and when members complete them, you need to record and store the data for future use in a format that is easily accessible and usable (such as transferring data from an electronic or paper survey to a spreadsheet). Additionally, if your CoP members are inexperienced with the chosen platform or tool, you may need to provide support and prompts to help people effectively complete the assessment.

### Case Study: Paola's Formal Assessment

Before each meeting of her CoP, Paola conducts a formal assessment by having all members register electronically. The registration form has questions about demographic information, such as a person's professional role and what organization she works for, and contact information. It then asks the person to answer several open-ended queries:

- What is one thing you hope to get out of this meeting?
- What challenges, if any, are you seeking support for?
- Do you have a resource, tool, or strategy to share during this meeting? If so, please describe it.
- What other comments or questions do you wish to share?

### Informal Methods

The following list presents some informal methods of collecting data.

- An email that invites members to give feedback on the proposed agenda for the next meeting, request that new items be added, or both
- A show of hands
- Small-group discussions
- Full-group discussions
- Reviewing the agenda at the beginning of a meeting and asking individuals to share their priorities
- Asking open-ended questions
- Using chat, yes-no, and other features of an online platform that support information gathering and engagement
- Closing discussions

Informal methods of gathering data take little time to set up, and they are cost-effective because they do not require special tools to collect information. Facilitators and members can often share and discuss immediate feedback while information is clear and fresh. Particularly when you collect data through a discussion, you can expand upon what others have shared and ask follow-up questions, and members may identify and expand upon thoughts that they might not have otherwise had. These conversations can also prime members' thoughts for further assessments that you might conduct later.

On the other hand, informal methods have their drawbacks. Because the data often comes to you in a variety of formats—verbal comments, short or detailed emails, text messages, and so on—you have to carefully track and document the responses you receive. As a result, it can be hard to analyze and use this data to evaluate the CoP over time.

### Case Study: Sergei's Informal Assessment

Sergei conducts an informal assessment by texting all members of his CoP one week before their next meeting: "Hi, guys! Just a reminder that our next meeting is on June 28 at 6:30 p.m. in the conference room at the library. If you have any agenda items or any other priorities you'd like to address during the meeting, let me know."

### Selecting Your Methods

When deciding whether to use formal or informal methods for gathering data, consider the purpose (what you want to know and why), what type of data (qualitative, quantitative, or both) you need to achieve that purpose, the resources available to you, and how you might want to use the data for future evaluations. For example, if you choose to ask the same questions of everyone before each meeting so you can track trends, topic requests, demographics, and so on, you may want to create a standard form or survey that you can easily customize before each meeting. In contrast, if you just want to quickly determine what the CoP members want to talk about at the beginning of a meeting, you can ask for a show of hands.

## Case Study: How Tuiara Collects and Uses Data

Tuiara facilitates a large CoP focused on practices that help improve child and family outcomes. Because her organization pays her a stipend for serving as the facilitator, she must collect, organize, and report data on the CoP: who participates in each meeting, the geographic regions from which members come, the topics discussed, the resources and strategies shared, the real or perceived effects of CoP participation on members' practices, new strategies that members apply, and so on.

Tuiara knows that she will have to thoroughly evaluate the data she gathers, so she chooses to use a combination of formal methods to collect information at various times. Before each meeting, she sends out an electronic registration form to all members. She takes notes during meetings and saves the chat logs from the CoP's online meeting room. At the end of each meeting, she holds a debriefing conversation with the members and writes down their responses to her questions. In the short term, Tuiara uses this information to plan for future meetings. For the long term, she compiles the data from each meeting into an overall spreadsheet so she and her organization can track how many strategies the members apply over time and can examine the real or perceived impact of those strategies.

### Sample Questions

If you are still unsure what questions to ask on an assessment, try customizing some of the questions in this section to match your purpose.*

#### Question 1

Mark your level of interest in exploring each of these topics (high, medium, or low).

| Topics | High Interest | Medium Interest | Low Interest |
|---|---|---|---|
| Working with families | ☐ | ☐ | ☐ |
| Using a certain curriculum (such as Montessori or Reggio Emilia) | ☐ | ☐ | ☐ |
| Handling challenging behaviors | ☐ | ☐ | ☐ |
| Working with children with special needs | ☐ | ☐ | ☐ |
| Other high priorities (please specify): ________ ________ | ☐ | ☐ | ☐ |

***Note:** All sample questions in this chapter are based on questions created by the CoP Development Group.

This sample question uses a rating-scale format, but you could also have members arrange a list of topics in order of priority or mark their top three choices. You can customize this question by inserting a list of topics that you already know are of interest to CoP members. Make sure to include a place where respondents can add their own ideas.

### Question 2

In what ways would you like to connect with others who share your interests? Select all that apply.

- ☐ Periodic online meetings
- ☐ Periodic in-person meetings
- ☐ Email list
- ☐ Online workspace (a place to share resources, troubleshoot, and problem solve with one another)
- ☐ Sharing resources (such as through a shared folder on Google Drive or Dropbox)
- ☐ Facebook
- ☐ Twitter
- ☐ Pinterest
- ☐ Other (please specify): ________________

________________________________________

This sample question gathers information about the ways in which members would like to connect with each other. Note that the options included in this question need to be customized and realistic for your CoP. For example, if the CoP members live near one another, it may be realistic to have in-person meetings. However, if CoP members work and live in different geographic regions and time zones, meetings may need to happen online, so you might ask the respondents to choose from among several platforms. Conversely, if you have no interest or skill in supporting member connections on, say, social media, then do not include social media as an option on your assessment—unless you plan to recruit a cofacilitator or another member of the CoP to help mediate such connections.

### Question 3

What are you hoping to gain from participating in this CoP?

- ☐ Connecting with other people who share my interests
- ☐ Hearing examples, tips, and strategies from other CoP members
- ☐ Having an opportunity to ask questions
- ☐ Sharing my knowledge and experiences
- ☐ Establishing a new network of supports that I can go to for help
- ☐ Identifying new resources I can use
- ☐ Identifying new strategies I can apply

Describe any other goals you hope to achieve for yourself, your practices, or your organization through participating in this CoP.

________________________________________

________________________________________

This sample question gathers information about what CoP members hope to gain as a result of their participation. You could instruct respondents to check all that apply or, if you need more-specific information, to choose only their top three priorities.

### Question 4

How frequently would you like to connect with other CoP members?

- ☐ Weekly
- ☐ Monthly
- ☐ Every other month
- ☐ Quarterly
- ☐ Other (please specify): ________________________________

This sample question gathers information about the frequency with which CoP members would like to connect. You could also ask other questions about the best lengths and times for meetings. Once again, consider what is realistic for the CoP and your ability to meet the needs that members may identify. If you cannot realistically do something (such as facilitating weekly meetings), omit that option from the assessment and substitute something more feasible, such as having CoP members email each other or share resources through a discussion board, a blog, social media, or an online workspace.

### Question 5

Rate what effect each of these things has on the success of the CoP.

| | Not Sure | No Effect | Some Effect | Significant Effect |
|---|---|---|---|---|
| Having a shared interest with CoP members | ☐ | ☐ | ☐ | ☐ |
| CoP members who value their participation | ☐ | ☐ | ☐ | ☐ |
| Opportunities to network with CoP members | ☐ | ☐ | ☐ | ☐ |
| Opportunities to network with outside professionals with different areas of expertise | ☐ | ☐ | ☐ | ☐ |
| Strong facilitator or facilitators | ☐ | ☐ | ☐ | ☐ |
| Effective communication that helps members stay engaged and informed | ☐ | ☐ | ☐ | ☐ |
| Multiple ways to participate (such as in-person meetings, phone calls, web conferences, email lists, and so on) | ☐ | ☐ | ☐ | ☐ |
| Frequencies and lengths of CoP meetings | ☐ | ☐ | ☐ | ☐ |
| Periodic evaluation of CoP's priorities and needs | ☐ | ☐ | ☐ | ☐ |
| Other (please specify): ____________ ____________ | ☐ | ☐ | ☐ | ☐ |

### Question 6

What are the greatest strengths of the CoP?

___

___

___

___

### Question 7

What suggestions, if any, do you have to make the CoP better?

___

___

___

___

These sample questions gather information about the quality of the CoP, the facilitation, and other resources that the group provides. For example, the facilitator is a driving force in the experiences that directly affect CoP members, so on an assessment, it is logical to include questions about the quality of facilitation. Facilitators may also be interested in learning more about what people think about the communication between meetings, the usefulness of online resources or sites used by the CoP, or the opportunity to network with others between calls. Really, any actions that may help the facilitator support the continuation of the CoP or improve her practices as a leader are valid for inclusion in an assessment.

## Determine When to Assess

Depending on the purpose of an assessment, you might conduct it once or repeatedly. For instance, if a meeting does not go well, you will ideally have to conduct only one assessment to find out what went wrong so you can keep the issue from occurring again. On the other hand, to keep track of members' demographics and needs, we (the authors) recommend that you use an assessment that collects this data (such as the surveys in appendices E and F) when your CoP is first established and at least once per year thereafter.

While the CoP as a whole should consider how often to conduct assessments, everyone also must be flexible, because occasionally the facilitator needs more information or needs it more frequently than usual to make decisions. For example, the facilitator might need to conduct an evaluation at any of the following times:

- When members' priorities become more diverse and the CoP seems at risk of splitting into subgroups
- When members show a lack of interest in CoP meetings and activities
- Annually to evaluate the CoP's value to and impact on members

Besides these less-frequent evaluations, facilitators have numerous opportunities for ongoing data collection through premeeting, real-time, and postmeeting assessments. These assessments make up the majority of the evaluation that goes on in a CoP, providing the regular flow of information that facilitators need to keep the CoP on course.

### Premeeting Assessment

*Premeeting assessment* takes place before a scheduled meeting and seeks data that helps the facilitator prepare effectively for that meeting. Some facilitators use premeeting assessment only if they get stuck while planning, but using this tool before each meeting—for example, by having members register, fill out a survey, or both—benefits both the facilitator and the CoP members. (See appendix G for a sample premeeting registration form and survey.) Wenger, McDermott, and Snyder assert that this practice helps the facilitator anticipate members' needs and manage her own expectations. For instance, using information from premeeting assessments, the facilitator can learn how many people to expect at each meeting and plan appropriate activities. A full-group discussion, for example, may not work well with twenty attendees.

The facilitator can also use the data from premeeting assessments to create agendas centered on the topics that members highlight and to decide how much time to spend on each item, thus giving the members ownership in how they spend meeting time. Furthermore, she can develop materials that members need and can find or create opportunities for CoP members to find useful tools and connect with other members, outside experts, or other professionals who can address members' questions and concerns. If the results of the premeeting assessment contain too many topics to address in one meeting, the facilitator can use the information to plan for future meetings.

#### Case Study: Using Premeeting Assessment to Plan Meetings

Deandre sends an email survey to his CoP members to determine what they want to discuss at next month's meeting. As the responses come in, Deandre finds that many people want to know more about how to use complex vocabulary with dual-language learners. As he considers how to meet this need, his colleague Kinaaz comes to mind. She can address this topic from both professional and personal experience—not only is she the director of a language-immersion preschool in which staff and students speak Spanish for 50 percent of the day, but she immigrated to the United States from Pakistan when she was two and learned English alongside Punjabi, her family's native language. Deandre emails Kinaaz with an invitation to attend next month's meeting and present some strategies for the CoP members to try.

Premeeting assessments can provide immense help to a facilitator, but they come with a few cautions. First, keep premeeting assessments simple. If you send out a lengthy, time-consuming survey before every meeting, CoP members may stop responding. Second, if people do take time to complete a premeeting assessment, make sure you review the responses and incorporate them into the agenda. Members will stay more engaged in the CoP in general and in the preassessment process specifically when they see that it is worth their while to provide feedback.

### Real-Time Assessment

*Real-time assessment* happens during a meeting. It seeks information about members' priorities and needs so that the facilitator can manage time and the agenda in the most useful way for members. Real-time assessment proves especially informative if not all members responded to a premeeting assessment or if the facilitator did not use one.

Additionally, real-time assessment helps set the tone for the meeting. It empowers participants to have a voice and help drive the discussion by getting them engaged as active contributors. In this way, it also cultivates interpersonal relationships and a sense of community. Furthermore, real-time assessment keeps everyone on task and in line with the shared interest. It can even lead members to identify other resources or supports to pursue outside of the CoP.

#### Beginning-of-Meeting Questions

One common method of real-time assessment is for the facilitator to spend the first few minutes of each meeting inquiring about what members hope to get out of their time together and what new priorities, if any, have arisen since the last meeting. She might ask questions such as the following:

- What brought you here today?
- What do you hope to accomplish by the end of the meeting?
- What new priorities do you want to address?
- What resources or supports do you seek from the CoP?
- Have you worked on or discovered anything that you would like to share with the group today?

A good facilitator builds time into meetings to gather this type of information and to then adapt the schedule accordingly.

#### Polling and Discussion Questions

Real-time assessment also occurs through the use of polling and discussion questions. Polling questions tend to work better for gathering quantitative information, while discussion questions typically work better for collecting qualitative information. Thus, the two types of questions make a powerful combination. For example, you could use a poll to gather quantitative information and then use a follow-up discussion to dig deeper.

You can include these activities at any point in a meeting to formally or informally gauge participants' interests and needs. For example, you might take a poll at the beginning of each meeting to determine members' professional roles and levels of experiences. You could also pose discussion questions to the entire group or to small groups. If your CoP meets in person, you might ask for a show of hands to choose a discussion topic from a list. You could also pose a question through a platform such as polleverywhere.com and have members submit responses from their cell phones. If your CoP meets virtually, try using the polling tools included in online platforms such as Adobe Connect, GoToMeeting, WebEx, and Zoom. If you prefer a more formal approach, you could create a "parking lot" (perhaps sheets of chart paper posted around the room for an in-person meeting or a shared document for a virtual meeting) where members can write their priorities or outstanding questions, which you then document in the meeting notes.

Regardless of how your CoP meets, polling works particularly well when you have a large group and insufficient time for everyone to voice her thoughts. Polls can collect anything from basic demographic information to details about experiences and preferences. If you want to examine overall results and see what the percentages are for each question, create a poll with multiple-choice questions; this option can help you determine, for example, how familiar the CoP members are with a topic or what subject they want to discuss. Try using some of the following questions, always making sure to include an "other" category with space for respondents to provide details:

- How many years have you been in the early childhood field? (provide options such as 0–6 months, 7–12 months, 1–3 years, and so on)
- What is your professional role? (list some roles that might apply to the members)
- What topic would you like to prioritize today? (list some topics related to the shared interest and practices)

A multiple-choice poll can also provide a fun and playful way to build connections between CoP members, especially in a virtual CoP with members from many locations. Try some of the following questions, making sure to include an "other" category for each:

- What is the weather like where you are? (warm, sunny, cold, snowing, rainy, windy, and so on)
- What is your favorite food? (Italian, Mexican, Chinese, pizza, seafood, cake, and so on)
- What is your ideal vacation? (beach, hiking, skiing, exploring Europe, and so on)

### Capturing Real-Time Assessment Data

Whether you use a poll, a chat feature, a sheet of chart paper, or some other medium to capture the results of a real-time assessment, remember to pay attention and periodically review that information during the meeting so it can guide you. After the meeting, document and store the information, perhaps as part of the meeting notes. You can also use it for later analysis to help plan future meetings and activities.

### Postmeeting Assessment

Postmeeting assessment seeks information about what did or did not go well during a meeting and what to do in future meetings. Postmeeting assessment can give the facilitator ideas for future meeting topics and show her any adjustments needed to keep the CoP true to the members' shared interests and practices. This type of evaluation also gives members a voice, allowing them to express what they liked or disliked and what they still need. Furthermore, it provides important information about what participants value and achieve as a result of their participation in the CoP.

Postmeeting assessments can use formal or informal methods. For instance, the facilitator might set aside the last five or ten minutes of every meeting for members to verbally summarize what they have learned, what they plan to try, what additional questions they have, and what other supports, strategies, resources, or activities they seek. This informal method gives the facilitator immediate feedback about the current meeting and allows each member to ask questions and suggest ideas for the next meeting. Alternatively, if time does not allow for a closing discussion or if the CoP members need time to process before giving feedback, the facilitator may choose to follow up more formally by distributing a short survey or questionnaire.

Regardless of format, postmeeting assessment questions might include the following:

- What is one thing you learned from the discussion?
- What is one thing you plan to try or apply as a result of your participation in the meeting?
- What other topics, resources, or supports do you seek from the CoP?
- What other comments, questions, or suggestions would you like to offer?

A facilitator might choose to use both formal and informal strategies for postmeeting assessment. She can close each meeting by gathering some informal feedback in a discussion and then follow up with a survey or questionnaire. If time permits and the two sets of questions are not too redundant, this technique may help the facilitator optimize the feedback she gathers, as each method of evaluation will likely produce some information that the other does not. (See appendix H for a sample postmeeting assessment in the form of a survey.)

### Capturing and Using Postmeeting Assessment Data

If you conduct a postmeeting assessment at the end of a meeting, make sure to document it in the meeting notes so you can revisit it when planning for future meetings and activities. You can also share this record with absent members to provide a summary of what they missed.

### Special Considerations for Formal Postmeeting assessment

A formal approach to collecting postmeeting feedback, such as using a survey or questionnaire, presents special benefits and challenges. Some of them appear in the following table.

| Benefits | Challenges |
|---|---|
| • May produce more-detailed responses than are possible during a discussion<br>• Collects information from people who might not speak during a group discussion<br>• Provides information that is easy to collect and document | • Members may not complete the evaluation if they have to find time outside the meeting to do it<br>• Paper evaluations may necessitate data entry later<br>• Members may not have technology access to complete an electronic evaluation outside the meeting |

It is often a struggle to get CoP members to complete a postmeeting assessment outside of a meeting. You can send reminders and prompts, but unless members have some incentive to fill out an assessment, they may not do so. To provide incentives, you could give certificates or, if you have the authority to do so, continuing education credits to members who complete assessments. On the other hand, if your CoP forms part of an ongoing professional-development opportunity, the supervising organization might require members to complete assessments to receive continuing education hours or credit for participating in meetings.

### Tip: Electronic Feedback in Virtual CoPs

Some online meeting rooms offer a feature that prompts participants to respond to electronic survey questions immediately following a meeting. The facilitator could also share a link to an electronic assessment in the chat feature. Collecting feedback right away can help with the response rate, as long as the facilitator explains during the meeting why she needs this feedback and then leaves some time at the end for people to complete the assessment.

# Chapter 5 Study Guide

## For Facilitators

How can you ask for meaningful feedback before, during, and after CoP meetings?

What kinds of information will you ask for, and why?

If you have little or no time for assessment during meetings, how can you create time for it?

## For Members

How do you share feedback with the facilitator and other members before, during, and after meetings?

If you do not have the opportunity to provide feedback, what happens to your level of engagement?

How might you communicate your interests and priorities to a facilitator if that information is not already being collected?

CHAPTER 6

# USING EVALUATION TO ENHANCE A COMMUNITY OF PRACTICE

Now that you have assessed your CoP, what do you do with the information you have gathered? Recall from chapter 5 that *evaluation* involves using collected data to monitor progress and make decisions. This chapter explains how to use evaluation to determine what direction a CoP should take, to improve the facilitator's skills, and to maximize the CoP's value for its members.

## Why Evaluate Your Assessment Data?

Without evaluation, assessment data is simply a collection of words, numbers, or both. Evaluation bridges the gap from *knowing* things about a CoP and its members to *doing* things to make sure that the CoP continues to meet members' needs.

One of the most important parts of evaluation is demonstrating the CoP's value and impact by showing its effects on its members and on the organizations and stakeholders they serve. This information also helps inform decisions about whether a CoP benefits individuals or organizations enough to warrant continuing the CoP. If your CoP formed organically, you may need to demonstrate these things only to its members; this information will likely help them stay engaged in the CoP. However, if an early childhood organization supports your CoP, the organization may need to gather additional information as part of its responsibility to report effects and achievements to stakeholders or other higher powers, such as program administrators, institutions of higher education, state early childhood advisory councils, or a state board of education. These groups may have decision-making power over what resources are available to sustain your CoP (such as staff time or access to online platforms), so it is important to show these groups how your CoP benefits its participants.

## Evaluating Your Assessment Data

### Looking for Patterns

To start the evaluation process, review your assessment data and look for patterns, which often clearly suggest how to act on your assessment data. For instance, perhaps you find a certain subject mentioned repeatedly as a topic of interest, so you might invite a guest speaker to present on the new interest. As another example, perhaps only a few people mark your CoP's current platform as their preferred way to connect with the group, so you might analyze the data further to see whether there is a clear preference for a specific alternative platform. If so, you might transition to using that platform; if not, you might conduct another assessment to get more information.

The value provided by CoP participation often appears in patterns, too. However, because these patterns can be difficult to spot and because they are critical to gaining support for continuing the CoP, we will treat them separately.

## Measuring Value

Measuring the value of individuals' participation in the CoP is relatively straightforward. Facilitators can collect this information directly from CoP members by asking them to provide feedback on the experiences they have had within the CoP and as a result of their participation. However, it can be more challenging to gather the information needed to determine a CoP's effect on an organization and other stakeholders, because there are more variables to consider and it may be impossible to account for all of them. Whether you are measuring a CoP's value to individuals or to organizations, it is essential to ask the right questions. The next few sections, which include sample questions*, can help you identify a CoP's value on many different levels.

Wenger, Trayner, and de Laat classify the value that a CoP provides into five categories:

- Immediate value
- Potential value
- Applied value
- Realized value
- Reframing value

### Immediate Value

Wenger, Trayner, and de Laat state that *immediate value* refers to the quality and relevance of activities that take place within the CoP. CoPs can provide immediate value when members connect over topics that are relevant to their interests and practices, engage in productive discussions, ask questions and answer each other's questions, and share and seek resources. If CoP members feel that group meetings are not relevant to their practices or are unproductive because the group does not keep on topic or on task, then people may not see it as worthwhile to participate. In contrast, if a CoP provides immediate value to its members, they will make time to participate, because they know that this is a place where they have the opportunity to engage in meaningful discussions and to identify and share resources.

***Note:** All sample questions in this chapter are based on Wenger, Trayner, and de Laat and the "Sample—CoP Participant Evaluation" by the CoP Development Group.

### Case Study: Immediate Value in Medina's CoP

A statewide committee forms a CoP for practitioners from various regions to help participants implement a new initiative connected to their State Systemic Improvement Plan (SSIP). Medina, who joins the group, finds that engaging and productive discussions enable the members to exchange ideas about how to recruit additional practitioners across their regions as they lead and support others who hope to improve their practices. Members of the CoP share tools and resources currently used in their regions and discuss ways these tools can be adapted to fit the unique needs of a particular region. The CoP meets every other month, and most meeting time is spent sharing practical strategies and problem solving with one another.

### Case Study: Immediate Value in Wilma's CoP

Wilma, an early interventionist, has decided to try to leave her toy bag in the car when she goes on home visits. She knows that she needs to learn more about each family's routines and work with them within the context of their natural environments. Wilma does not have a coach or supervisor to help her with these practices, so she has joined a CoP with other practitioners whom she met at a recent training session. They have all relied on their toy bags for years, and the CoP has become a place for Wilma, among others, to share stories about her experiences without her toy bag and then receive feedback from her colleagues. Wilma has found immediate value in her participation because she gains support and ideas she can try immediately. She is also gaining confidence, as she sometimes gets to be the one who provides tips and strategies to others in the CoP based on the approaches she has tried and the lessons she has learned from her experiences.

### Case Study: Immediate Value in Oscar's CoP

A group of teachers and practitioners in an online CoP swap experiences, resources, and contact information for potential new recruits as they work to understand and apply the Division for Early Childhood's (DEC's) Recommended Practices in their work. Oscar, the facilitator, moderates the discussion board and provides resources, guiding questions, and prompts when the dialogue appears to go off topic. This helps ensure that discussions are always relevant to the shared interest and practices of CoP members. This is also a place where CoP members can ask questions and get timely support from their fellow members.

### Sample Questions

When assessing the immediate value of your CoP, try using the following questions.

Rate the quality of each of these types of interactions in your CoP.

| | Does Not Occur | Poor | Fair | Average | Very Good | Excellent |
|---|---|---|---|---|---|---|
| Productive discussions among members | ☐ | ☐ | ☐ | ☐ | ☐ | ☐ |
| Members getting answers to questions | ☐ | ☐ | ☐ | ☐ | ☐ | ☐ |
| Members sharing experiences | ☐ | ☐ | ☐ | ☐ | ☐ | ☐ |
| Members sharing resources or connections | ☐ | ☐ | ☐ | ☐ | ☐ | ☐ |

Rate the relevance of your CoP activities and interactions to your work.

☐ Poor
☐ Fair
☐ Average
☐ Very good
☐ Excellent

### Potential Value

According to Wenger, Trayner, and de Laat, *potential value* refers to information gained from a CoP that may not be useful just yet but can help members later. CoPs create potential value as members learn new skills, establish new relationships, receive ongoing access to resources to support their work, and gain recognition from other members, their own supervisors, or their peers outside the CoP. Every CoP provides a network of supports for its members, because every person in the CoP brings different experiences and expertise to the group. For example, Feodora immigrated to the United States as a young child and speaks fluent Russian. While none of her fellow CoP members has an immediate need for assistance with the Russian language or culture, this relationship has potential value for any CoP member who might later need to rely on Feodora's experience or expertise.

### Case Study: Potential Value in Umberto's CoP

Umberto belongs to a virtual CoP with members from all over the United States. The CoP's shared interest is helping new students successfully become part of their classroom communities. Umberto's fellow members have helped him tremendously as he's worked with many newcomers to his class, but now he has a new student with a challenge that he's never encountered before: she suffered lead poisoning as an infant and, as a result, has difficulty learning. Umberto does not know how to help her, so he turns to his CoP. Several members live in states that have set policies to secure services for children who have been exposed to lead, and these members offer Umberto resources, suggestions for whom else to consult, and advice. No one had predicted this particular need, but when it arose, Umberto knew that he could get help by relying on the potential value in the knowledge and experience of his fellow CoP members.

### Case Study: Potential Value in Oscar's CoP

In Oscar's CoP, most members spend the majority of their CoP time reading various threads on the discussion board, going back and forth as they soak up ideas and write down things they want to try. One thread has particularly high potential value because it is dedicated to spreading the word about upcoming learning opportunities, such as training events, webinars, and conferences. Similarly, the relationships among CoP members have potential value because individuals know that whenever they need to ask new questions or seek support for trying different strategies, Oscar and their fellow members will be there to support them.

### Sample Question

When assessing the potential value of your CoP, try using the following question.

| From My Participation in My CoP . . . | Strongly Disagree | Disagree | Neither Agree nor Disagree | Agree | Strongly Agree |
|---|---|---|---|---|---|
| I have gained new knowledge and skills. | ☐ | ☐ | ☐ | ☐ | ☐ |
| I feel more confident and motivated to do my work. | ☐ | ☐ | ☐ | ☐ | ☐ |
| I have developed new relationships with colleagues. | ☐ | ☐ | ☐ | ☐ | ☐ |
| I feel supported in my role and feel that I can turn to CoP members for assistance. | ☐ | ☐ | ☐ | ☐ | ☐ |
| I have access to resources and information that I would not have easily obtained from another source. | ☐ | ☐ | ☐ | ☐ | ☐ |

### Applied Value

Wenger, Trayner, and de Laat explain *applied value* as a change in practice that results from participating in a CoP. Applied value could include any of the following actions:

- Implementing a new idea or strategy
- Using knowledge gained from the CoP to help inform a decision
- Contacting a fellow member for support outside of a CoP meeting
- Adapting a resource (either from the CoP or, with permission, from another group) to support an individual's or group's unique needs
- Sharing resources gained outside the CoP (such as from outside training, web research, or organizations in which members work) with other CoP members
- Inviting others to join the CoP

For example, a preschool teacher might use an activity created by another CoP member, or an administrator might change his program's procedures based on something he learned within a CoP.

### Case Study: Applied Value in Umberto's CoP

Umberto accepts and learns from the materials and examples provided by his fellow CoP members. Over time, he uses and adapts these resources to help develop policies in his state for providing services to children who have been exposed to lead.

### Case Study: Applied Value in Valerie's CoP

Valerie belongs to a CoP of professional-development specialists and technical-assistance providers. As they discuss their concerns and shared interests, they realize that they are all teaching the same concepts according to the same federal laws and regulations. They pool their resources and jointly develop materials that can be adapted and applied nationwide to serve many audiences for a variety of purposes.

### Case Study: Applied Value in Wilma's CoP

Wilma finally feels confident enough to leave her toy bag at home, not just in her car, when she goes to perform home visits. She also invites some of her colleagues to join the CoP.

### Sample Questions

When assessing the applied value of your CoP, try using the following questions.

Which of these things have you done because of your participation in the CoP? Select all that apply.

- ☐ I have applied information or skills that I acquired in the CoP.
- ☐ I have used documents and resources that someone shared in the CoP.
- ☐ I have contacted someone from the CoP as a resource or for mutual support.
- ☐ I have collaborated with someone from the CoP on a joint project.
- ☐ I have shared resources from the CoP with others outside the CoP.
- ☐ I have told others about the CoP.
- ☐ I have invited someone to join the CoP.
- ☐ Other (please specify): ____________________

____________________

- ☐ None of the above

Use the following space to briefly summarize your experience with each item you selected.

____________________

____________________

____________________

____________________

____________________

### Realized Value

*Realized value*, according to Wenger, Trayner, and de Laat, is performance change, whether on a small scale or a large one. This is one step beyond applied value, because changing a *practice* does not necessarily mean that overall *performance* improves. Realized value requires reflection on what, if anything, has been affected by what was applied. This could include looking at individual accomplishments and the value and effects the CoP has had on an organization or stakeholders served by the CoP members. Sometimes realized value becomes apparent through self-reflective activities, reflections, and observations with a supervisor or mentor. In other cases, it appears in statements from stakeholders who recognize and benefit from the applicable changes.

### Case Study: Realized Value in Andelina's CoP

A real-life early interventionist, whom we'll call Andelina, began using family-centered practices and made teamwork and collaboration with her colleagues a greater priority because of what she had learned in CoP activities. Andelina started to let families lead the intervention visits she had with them, and she met them in a variety of settings where they felt that they needed more support, such as grocery stores and favorite restaurants. She even scheduled periodic evening and weekend visits so she could teach and model strategies for other caregivers as needed. Andelina also made an effort to routinely connect with other providers along the way to share strategies and successes.

Andelina realized that these changes improved her relationships with the families she served, and she found great benefits from the stronger bonds she formed with the other practitioners on her team. Her supervisor also recognized what was happening, and at a staff meeting, she asked Andelina to share with her peers what she had learned and applied.

### Case Study: Realized Value in Valerie's CoP

The materials created by Valerie's CoP can affect individuals, organizations, and stakeholders at local, statewide, national, and international levels. In this case, realized value may become visible when the individuals who developed the materials are recognized by their supervisors, peers, fellow CoP members, and employers. When the materials are distributed and used at various levels, organizations may realize value in the funds they have saved by not having to develop materials on their own. Realized value also shows itself when people who use or receive instruction from the materials report their experiences and changes in practice. Realized value may come about when states across a nation and countries around the globe begin to access the resources and invite CoP members to international conferences to speak on how to use the materials.

The examples could go on and on, but you can see how realized value can be individualized or transcend the CoP, affecting organizations and stakeholders on a much larger scale.

### Sample Questions

When assessing the realized value of your CoP, try using the following questions.

What recognition and achievements have you acquired because of your participation in the CoP? Select all that apply.

- ☐ I have received positive feedback from a peer or supervisor on new tools I have used or shared.
- ☐ I have received positive feedback from a peer or supervisor on new skills I have demonstrated.
- ☐ I have a new network of supports that would have otherwise been difficult to establish.
- ☐ I have achieved something new in my role, such as a job opportunity, a promotion, or opportunities to lead.
- ☐ I have helped affect or contribute to programmatic changes, organizational changes, or both at a local, state, or national level.
- ☐ Other (please specify): ____________________

____________________

- ☐ None of the above

Use the following space to briefly summarize your experience with each item you selected.

____________________

____________________

____________________

____________________

____________________

How effective has the CoP been in helping you do the following things in your role within the early childhood community?

| | N/A | Ineffective | Slightly Effective | Somewhat Effective | Moderately Effective | Very Effective |
|---|---|---|---|---|---|---|
| Support local initiatives | ☐ | ☐ | ☐ | ☐ | ☐ | ☐ |
| Support statewide initiatives | ☐ | ☐ | ☐ | ☐ | ☐ | ☐ |
| Support national initiatives | ☐ | ☐ | ☐ | ☐ | ☐ | ☐ |

### Reframing Value

According to Wenger, Trayner, and de Laat, *reframing value* becomes visible when participation in the CoP causes individuals, programs, or organizations to redefine their strategies, goals, and values. This process involves transforming or leaving behind old practices to implement new definitions, standards, or measures of success—or all three. For example, as a result of participating in a CoP, one early childhood program decided that it could not call itself high quality unless it used inclusive practices for young children with disabilities. In another case, because of their participation in a CoP, members of a state department of education concluded that the state should redefine its early learning guidelines, and they began to advocate for this change.

#### Case Study: Reframing Value in Andelina's CoP

In real life, Andelina's story shows reframing value at an individual level. She decided to hold herself to a new standard as she worked to learn and apply family-centered practices and to be a better collaborator and team member. She drew from the immediate, potential, applied, and realized value she had gained from her CoP and made a plan to move forward. It was a major shift in her goals for herself and her practices, and it took time to master, but she committed to the change and followed through.

### Sample Questions

When assessing the reframing value of your CoP, try using the following questions.

Which of the following results have occurred because of your participation in your CoP? Select all that apply.

- ☐ I am thinking about trying something new in my practice.
- ☐ I am setting new goals for myself and my practice.
- ☐ I am trying or applying something new in my practice.
- ☐ I am changing the way that I think about or approach my work.
- ☐ I am reframing or changing the way I have always done something.
- ☐ Other (please specify): ____________________
- ☐ None of the above

Use the following space to briefly summarize your experience with each item you selected.

____________________

____________________

____________________

____________________

## Using Data to Make CoP Improvements

Data on the impact of a CoP can help the facilitator and the members decide how to move the CoP from perceived impact ("I think it might help my work someday") to actual impact ("I have changed my practice in specific ways because of my participation in this group"). To understand the data related to impact, the facilitator must also recognize where the CoP is in its life cycle and understand what level of impact she can reasonably expect at that stage. According to Wenger, Trayner, and de Laat, members of newer CoPs tend to rate their groups as having potential impact, because the information they are receiving in the CoP is new to them and they have not had sufficient time to truly make lasting changes. Conversely, members of longer-standing CoPs tend to rate their groups as having had actual impact on their practices—they have had more time and more experience with group problem solving and sharing, which have helped them hone their practices and make real and lasting changes in their work. On the other hand, if a longer-standing group continues to rate the impact of the CoP as potential (that is, they believe that it can help them change but hasn't done so yet), the facilitator may want to consider having a whole-CoP discussion or interviews with individuals to get their ideas for how to move the group along. Additionally, the facilitator should consider this data along with the feedback on his own skill and effectiveness as a facilitator; changes in his approach or process could help the CoP begin to have more actual than potential impact.

## Reviewing Results with CoP Members

After conducting any assessment in his CoP and analyzing the data, the facilitator needs to summarize and report the results to the CoP's members. There are several important reasons to do so:

- First, though many group members may provide similar answers on evaluations and assessments, sharing results enables all members to learn about others' perspectives and provides opportunities for members to expand upon or clarify their answers.
- Similarly, the facilitator may need to discuss some areas of an assessment with the members so he and they can understand the results, such as when many individuals say that the time of the meetings is not convenient but do not indicate on the survey what alternative schedule might be better. The facilitator may want to ask questions to determine whether a change is really needed or whether the members are currently very busy and feel overwhelmed no matter what time the CoP meets. Sharing and discussing data also goes a long way toward showing the members that the facilitator listens to them and wants to make changes that work for the CoP.
- Finally, if the CoP has experienced major transitions such as leadership change or membership shifts, assessment data may yield important information that will help the group stay connected and focused—that is, if everyone knows about that information.

After collecting assessment data and analyzing them, the facilitator can easily share the results of the survey by converting the responses into an easy-to-read-and-digest format, such as a one-page summary, and distributing it to the CoP members. Then the group can have a review meeting, in which they spend part or all of the meeting discussing the summary and making joint decisions about next steps. Before the review meeting, the facilitator should use the responses to develop a few discussion questions so he can gather additional information from the members. Here are some ideas:

- What do you think about meeting more frequently or less frequently? Would that continue to meet our needs?
- [Insert applicable person's name], you mentioned that you want to talk more about [insert topic]. Please explain more about what you would like to know or discuss.
- Do some people want to hold separate discussions about [insert topic]? Or should we continue to address it as a full group?
- Some people mentioned wanting to develop a resource on [insert topic]. Who would want to work on this? How could we accomplish this?

During a review meeting, as the group comes to an understanding of what the results mean, the facilitator identifies what decisions need to be made, solicits possible choices from the members, and facilitates discussion about them. Using this input, the facilitator determines what adjustments to make and secures commitment from the members to make those changes. But what might those changes be? They commonly involve alterations in the CoP's structure or approach to discussing topics, but the details depend on the type of assessment used and the information it produces.

### Off-Topic Results

Sometimes assessment reveals a need or interest that differs widely from the shared interests of the CoP. In these cases, the facilitator may want to identify applicable resources and supports and share them with the appropriate person outside of regular meetings so as not to disrupt the priorities of the larger group. If several CoP members show strong interest in the same off-topic subject, the facilitator could suggest that these members form a subgroup so that they can still participate in the CoP while exploring their other mutual interest on their own time.

## Deciding How to Act on Assessment and Evaluation Results

Once you (the facilitator) and your CoP have discussed the results of an assessment or evaluation, you collectively need to decide what to do to make the improvements you have identified. Sometimes you can clearly see what actions to take, as in many of the examples in this chapter. But if you get stuck, the following table suggests some ideas. You do not have to take all the listed actions after every assessment; select the ones that seem the most reasonable for the questions you have asked in a given assessment and the results you have gained through analyzing the data.

| Concern | Possible Actions |
|---|---|
| Frequency of meetings | • Meet more frequently if members need more time with the CoP.<br>• Meet less frequently if attendance is dwindling or inconsistent. |
| Type of meetings | • Switch partly or entirely to in-person meetings.<br>• Switch partly or entirely to virtual meetings. |
| Platforms | • If the members mention having difficulty with the current platform, consider using alternative platforms, such as conference calling or web-based video.<br>• If members mention issues with accessing a physical meeting space, such as if the address is difficult to find or parking is limited, consider finding a new location. |
| Topics | • Explore possible subtopics.<br>• Revisit topics that the CoP has already discussed.<br>• Explore tangential yet related topics to deepen participants' understanding of the shared interest. |
| Format of meetings | • Increase or decrease the number of presentations by outside experts.<br>• Increase or decrease the number of presentations by members.<br>• Increase or decrease the number of member-led discussions. |
| Online shared space | • Ensure that the space is functional and useful to members.<br>• Determine whether members need additional support to access and use the space. |
| Joint-work products | • Determine the usefulness of any products the CoP has already developed. For example, do they need revising?<br>• Examine the need for the CoP to create additional products or tools. |
| Effectiveness of facilitation | • Add a cofacilitator.<br>• Have members facilitate parts of meetings.<br>• Change facilitators. |

The next several sections give some examples of decisions that facilitators and members can make based on the data from an assessment.

### Adjusting Logistics

When an assessment asks questions about meeting times, dates, durations, and formats (virtual or in person), the answers give insight into attendance patterns and possible changes needed in the CoP's logistics.

#### Case Study: Using an Assessment to Adjust Meeting Format

Precious has noticed attendance dwindling in her in-person CoP. She conducts an assessment, which reveals that the days and times of the meetings no longer work for many members because of transportation difficulties. During a review meeting, Precious and the members discuss how they might address this issue. One person suggests holding virtual meetings so that members who lack transportation can still attend. Precious agrees to research some online-meeting options and report her findings to the group by next week.

#### Case Study: Using an Assessment to Troubleshoot Tools

Gregorio's virtual CoP has struggled with its conference-call meetings. In his most recent assessment, members have complained about poor sound quality and other recurring technical difficulties during calls, especially for people using cell phones instead of landlines. The group discusses this problem in a review meeting. One member, Burhan, offers to consult his cousin, who works for a cell-phone company, for ideas about how individual members can troubleshoot during calls. Gregorio also volunteers to look into video-calling platforms as another possible solution.

### Restructuring Meetings

Assessment data may reveal a need to examine how the facilitator prepares agendas or how meetings run. For example, CoP members may indicate that they want to hear more from one another, whether through discussions or presentations, than from outside experts. This helps the facilitator plan the structure of meetings to spend more time on group sharing or presentations by members.

### Case Study: Using Assessments to Replan a Meeting

Xenia facilitates a CoP focused on the implementation of an early math curriculum. According to an assessment she conducted recently, some members have past experience with this curriculum and are very skilled in using it, but many of the newer members are feeling overwhelmed and lack confidence. Xenia had planned to invite a guest speaker, the statewide coordinator in charge of implementing the curriculum, to present to the CoP at their next meeting, but she realizes that the new members would likely feel even more bewildered at the end of what is likely to be a highly technical, detailed presentation. Instead, for the next meeting, Xenia has the experienced members of the group share how they have implemented the curriculum, how they have overcome roadblocks, and what supports they continue to need to hone their practice.

### Changing Discussion Topics

A CoP's shared interest or practice can vary throughout the life cycle of the CoP. In many cases, the facilitator and members simply turn their attention to different nuances of the topic or subtopics. For example, a CoP that initially focuses on measuring child outcomes in general may narrow its scope to measuring child outcomes in preschool special education. In other cases, the group might need to make broader changes, such as adjusting the specific focus within the shared interest or exploring additional, related topics. For instance, a CoP that started by studying social-emotional learning may opt to home in on supporting individual children's abilities to regulate their emotions.

Whether the topic changes significantly or slightly, assessments should regularly ask for input on additional topics of interest so the facilitator can plan which subjects to cover and at which meetings. This practice of regularly checking in also helps the facilitator to identify CoP members who can share information on certain topics and to decide whether to invite outside experts to present to the group. For example, in one virtual CoP, the facilitators used the information they gathered from a semiannual assessment to plan six to nine months of meetings in advance, including the sequence of topics, which members to ask to share information, and which presentations from other members or outside experts might help the members.

### Case Study: Using an Assessment to Find Presenters

Pam facilitates a CoP focused on child assessment. The group has been exploring the use of a particular curriculum-based assessment, but many of the recent group calls indicate that the CoP members want to branch out into other aspects of assessment.

To find out which specific aspects to pursue, Pam creates an assessment with a short list of potential topics for discussion in the coming months and asks the CoP members to rank the topics according to their own priorities and to add any desired topics that are not on the list. After reviewing the results, Pam drafts a potential order of topics for discussion in the next six calls. Several of the topics relate to professional projects that some CoP members have worked on outside the group, so Pam reaches out to these members to determine whether they would be willing to share their current work.

The group's number-one topic choice is the functional assessment of young children with disabilities. Pam contacts CoP member Shamira, who has done a great deal of work in this area at the child-care center she owns. Shamira has created an observation tool to provide feedback to her staff, and she has heard from the teachers in her program about how the observations and the feedback are helping them think about changing their practices in functional assessment. Pam hopes that Shamira can speak at the first scheduled call, because several of the members' other topics of interest—observing young children and talking with families—flow naturally from what Shamira would share. Pam also considers reaching out to her old professor, Dr. Miller, who taught her graduate class on assessment and is regarded as a local expert, but she decides to wait until after Shamira responds.

## Determining the Next Steps in the CoP's Life Cycle

Assessment information can help the facilitator determine whether members still need the CoP, whether it needs to evolve into something different, or whether it has outlived its usefulness.

- If the CoP is still needed, the assessment indicates a high level of interest in topics, and individuals volunteer to share their work or can articulate how the CoP continues to support their professional growth. The overall results of the assessment show that the members feel positive and passionate about having continued meetings.
- If the CoP needs to evolve into something else, the assessment results will likely be mixed. Some of the participants may indicate mild to moderate interest in suggested topics by placing them neither very high nor very low when asked to rank them in order of preference. Other members, however, still are very excited about the existing topics and continue to suggest ideas because they still have high levels of interest and don't want the CoP to stop meeting. The overall response rate for the assessment may also be relatively low, or the facilitator may need to remind participants multiple times to complete it. In this case, it may be wise to capitalize on the topics that continue to generate excitement and use them as the basis of the new shared interest.

- If the community has outlived its usefulness, the assessment will clearly show it. Few or no members respond to it in the first place, or the overwhelming message from the members' feedback is that the CoP no longer brings value to their work.

The assessment may also provide more specific information within these categories. Based on members' responses, for example, the facilitator may learn that the group still wants to hold ongoing discussions about the same shared interest but perhaps wants to do so less frequently. Or the members may indicate that they would like to stay in touch via a shared space, such as a CoP website or an online discussion board, but have no need to meet on a regular basis.

### Improving Facilitation Quality

Assessment data and evaluation results provide a facilitator with important information about the ways in which he runs and supports his CoP. He must gather and review this information regularly because it also indicates the CoP's level of impact on its members (which we will discuss in a moment). If a facilitator discovers that members do not notice the CoP having any effect on their own practices, one of his first considerations should be how his facilitation contributes to the CoP. Even if the members do see the CoP making a difference in their work, they might need something different from the facilitator than he currently provides. For instance, an evaluation might show that a facilitator lacks some of the essential skills or characteristics discussed in chapter 4, but the results can also help him discover what improvements to make. After critical reflection, a facilitator might decide to recruit another facilitator to share responsibilities, or he might practice giving more time for people to think before he adds information to the discussion. On the other hand, if a facilitator leaves his job or changes job responsibilities and can no longer facilitate, the CoP will need a new facilitator altogether. At this point, it might help to ask the CoP members what characteristics they would like to have in their next facilitator or even if they have a nominee in mind.

### Connecting to Other Professional-Development Evaluations

When a facilitator uses the results of evaluation as part of *continuous quality improvement* (which we will discuss in a moment), he can decide how to manage and improve the CoP within a larger context of many professional-development activities. Most importantly, the results of these evaluations can show what it takes to learn, apply, and master new practices within the day-to-day work of an early childhood professional. Using this data, the facilitator might adjust discussion topics, meeting frequencies, or the foci of joint activities to support the members' application and mastery of information. A CoP should not often be the sole mechanism for members' professional development; it should be part of a combination of professional-development activities that may also include training, workshops, and coaching or mentoring from others. The evaluation results from the CoP may yield information that can be used not only to tweak and improve the CoP itself but also to inform the topics of future training opportunities or to determine the foci of individual mentoring sessions and support. The facilitator may opt to share aggregate data (instead of individual responses, thus maintaining members' privacy) from his CoP with the leaders of other professional-development activities so that together, they can plan the best ways to support practitioners' learning, application, and mastery of improved practices.

## Using CoPs as Part of Continuous Quality Improvement

You may have noticed something familiar about the process of regularly asking questions and then collecting, analyzing, and using evaluation data to make changes in your CoP. In fact, it greatly resembles the process of *continuous quality improvement* (CQI), which professionals use to make data-informed decisions at all levels of early childhood systems. CQI is a recurring cycle of identifying questions that need answering, making changes, collecting data to answer the questions, and analyzing the data to see what it reveals about the changes that you've made. In the report *Continuous Quality Improvement in Early Childhood and School-Age Programs*, Billie Young further defines CQI in early childhood education as "a process which ensures that organizations and their partners are systemic and intentional about improving services and practices and increasing positive outcomes for children and families."

Young explains that a typical improvement plan in an early childhood system focuses on having practitioners change a single aspect of their work. CQI allows them to go beyond this artificial limit. When decision-makers use CQI, they create a culture that encourages regularly working on quality improvements. In this type of environment, as the National Center for Educational Statistics asserts, decision-makers can continually identify and make systemic and organization-specific program improvements to lead to higher-quality services for young children and their families.

If you think that all of this sounds like what happens in a CoP, you are right. CoPs make excellent means for pursuing CQI, and CQI processes can benefit any CoP, even one that functions separately from formal CQI efforts. Let's examine one way in which the latter can happen.

### The Plan, Do, Study, Act Cycle

According to the National Implementation Research Network, improvement uses many different models, including the Plan, Do, Study, Act (PDSA) cycle. In this model, as the National Center for Educational Statistics explains, practitioners use data to select which improvements to pursue, to track whether practitioners effectively implement those changes, and to demonstrate whether the changes bring about the intended outcomes for children and families. The PDSA cycle works best when leaders and staff share a vision for what the improvements and the expected outcomes of those improvements will be.

**The Plan, Do, Study, Act Model**

**Plan.** Once a change or improvement is identified, plan for its implementation and identify ways to measure outcomes.

**Do.** Put implementation supports (e.g., new policies, professional development) in place; carry out the change or improvement as planned.

**Study.** Gather and analyze the data for outcomes and fidelity to implementation; consider any needed adjustments.

**Act.** Determine what modifications should be made, whether the change should be adopted or abandoned, and what else needs to be learned or completed. Then begin the cycle again.

**Source:** National Center for Educational Statistics, Institute of Education Sciences. 2017. *SLDS Issue Brief: Using ECIDS Data to Support Continuous Quality Improvement*. Issue brief. Washington, DC: National Center for Educational Statistics, Institute of Education Sciences. https://nces.grads360.org/services/PDCService.svc/GetPDCDocumentFile?fileId=28616. Used with permission.

Any group, including a CoP, can use the PDSA cycle to continue to improve an effort that they have already started. For example, a CoP can use the PDSA cycle to evaluate its own effectiveness, impact, and value. The facilitator regularly collects data on CoP members' needs, the CoP's perceived and real impact, and the efficacy of the group's functioning, and he shares all this information with the members. Based on the results, the entire group can decide what improvements to make. After implementing the changes, the group can then study those improvements to decide whether they have had the desired effects.

### Case Study: Using the PDSA Model

A CoP has formed among a group of teachers who are implementing a new social-emotional curriculum in their program. The plan is to start using the curriculum in ten of the twenty classrooms and then to gradually introduce it more widely. The first ten teachers collect data on the implementation and bring it to their CoP for everyone to examine. Using these findings, the CoP members recommend some adjustments to the implementation process, and they decide what additional data to collect to determine what difference the curriculum is making for the children in their classrooms. These changes are incorporated into the overall implementation plan beginning with the next five classrooms. After six months of using the new curriculum in all twenty classrooms, the CoP checks in to review additional data and to determine what next steps they should take.

This example illustrates how the PDSA cycle works well for a CoP, whether to manage a new initiative or to investigate a shared interest or practice. The freedom to explore data and to hear anecdotal information from other participants makes a CoP a natural support to any continuous quality improvement effort.

Whether or not your CoP operates within a CQI initiative, the PDSA cycle can support your CoP's health and well-being. After all, a CoP that does not meet members' needs also does not have much effect on application or mastery of skills and therefore will have little to no value to members. The PDSA cycle ensures that the facilitator and the members regularly and deliberately discuss the CoP's functioning and how it must adapt to continue to meet members' needs. This practice allows for frequent course corrections and improvements to the CoP's effectiveness.

# Chapter 6 Study Guide

What format would work best to share assessment results with your CoP (a short summary, charts and graphs, something else)?

How far in advance of the review meeting will you send assessment results to your CoP members so they can read them before the meeting?

What assessment results need clarification from the group? For example, you may wish to discuss questions in which members rated something lower than you expected or in which individual responses frequently disagreed with each other.

What questions will you ask to get the clarification needed?

What questions will you ask to determine what modifications to make to the CoP? Consider questions about the frequency of meetings, the topics covered, the format or structure of meetings, or additional supports, such as new products (for instance, articles, books, or guidance documents) or outside experts.

How often does your CoP look at or discuss data?

How does your CoP make decisions about changes or improvements?

# APPENDIX A: CREATING SPACE FOR MUTUAL ENGAGEMENT, JOINT ENTERPRISE, AND A SHARED REPERTOIRE

This worksheet is for facilitators of CoPs that are beginning to form. To create a CoP that is committed to exploring a topic or practice in depth, you will need to create space for mutual engagement, joint enterprise, and a shared repertoire. Use the following table to write down your initial ideas for how to do this. You can return to this table later to add more details.

| CoP Element | What This Element Involves | What Will You Do to Promote This Element? | What Resources or Supports Will You Need? |
|---|---|---|---|
| Mutual engagement | Interactions to share information, work together, and learn from one another | | |
| Joint enterprise | Working together toward a common goal | | |
| Shared repertoire | Developing and maintaining tools and resources | | |

# APPENDIX B: STRUCTURE AND FORMATTING CONSIDERATIONS FOR YOUR COMMUNITY OF PRACTICE

This worksheet is for facilitators of CoPs that are beginning to form. Circle the group structures or formats that you have used in the past. Star the ones that you think might work well for your CoP.

- Regular informal check-ins during which individual members identify topics they want to put on the agenda for a scheduled meeting
- Peer-led training sessions on a topic of interest to all members, in which a group member trains everyone else or leads a discussion
- Presentations on existing practices, followed by discussions on how to improve them
- Identification of problems for the group to discuss and solve together
- Combination of all of the above

How frequently will your CoP meetings occur? How long will they be? What format will you use (such as a conference call, video chat, or in-person meeting)?

______________________________________________

______________________________________________

______________________________________________

Create a meeting schedule here, including times and dates.

______________________________________________

______________________________________________

______________________________________________

What roles or jobs do you need in the CoP? Who will fill them?

______________________________________________

______________________________________________

______________________________________________

How will the CoP share and store resources?

______________________________________________

______________________________________________

______________________________________________

# APPENDIX C: LOGISTICS CHECKLIST FOR A VIRTUAL COMMUNITY OF PRACTICE

This checklist is for facilitators of CoPs that meet virtually. Use it to help you keep track of logistical concerns that are specific to this type of CoP.

- ☐ Investigate multiple types of online platforms that you can use to connect CoP members, such as video conferencing, conference-call lines, or web conference platforms. Select one that matches your budget, technology access (for example, do you have access to the internet and phone lines?), and computer equipment (for instance, do you have computers with newer processors or multiple monitors?).
- ☐ Spend time before scheduled meetings to learn about the functions and features of your chosen platform. If available, watch or participate in the vendor's demonstration of the features.
- ☐ Set regular dates and times for meetings, and send out calendar invitations that include these details and working links to the platform.
- ☐ Sign on fifteen minutes before each meeting to check sound quality and to connect with any members who will share materials during the meeting. Make sure those people know how to work the platform.
- ☐ If the platform allows, upload materials ahead of time and test whether you can share them with members.
- ☐ If you plan to use a poll during a meeting, develop and test it ahead of time.
- ☐ Develop a troubleshooting sheet for participants to solve initial issues with sound, video, or connection. If possible, have a designated technical-support person available to deal with these issues. This person can be a CoP facilitator, a CoP member, or another person from your organization who has knowledge of the system you use. If professional technical support is available, that is even better!
- ☐ Have a backup plan in case the technology fails on the day of a meeting, such as providing a conference-call number to call if your webinar software goes down.

# APPENDIX D: LOGISTICS CHECKLIST FOR AN IN-PERSON COMMUNITY OF PRACTICE

This checklist is for facilitators of CoPs that meet in person. Use it to help you keep track of logistical concerns that are specific to this type of CoP.

- ☐ Start with setting dates for meetings. Use feedback from the group to find the time and day that work best for the majority of the group.
- ☐ Send email invitations to CoP members with dates, times, and meeting locations. As needed, include physical addresses, contact phone numbers, and directions.
- ☐ Identify a meeting location that suits your needs both for size and costs. Options may include space in a building in which all the members work; centralized locations, such as an agency's state headquarters; or locations in the wider community, such as community centers, police-station meeting rooms, libraries, or hotels.
- ☐ Make sure that your location has all the equipment you need (such as a projector, screen, or phone) for your meeting.
- ☐ Make a virtual connection possible for those that may not be able to attend in person. For example, reserve a conference-call line or set up a meeting in Zoom, and send all CoP members the necessary information to join the virtual meeting. Even members who usually attend in person may encounter last-minute emergencies that prevent them from being physically present.
- ☐ Prepare all materials, such as handouts, slides, and resources, prior to the meeting, and make copies as needed.
- ☐ Arrive thirty minutes prior to the meeting to set up the room to facilitate discussion. Make note of the room's arrangement, such as by taking a photo, before you start.
- ☐ Return the room to its original setup before you leave.

# APPENDIX E: SAMPLE ANNUAL NEEDS-ASSESSMENT AND IMPACT SURVEY

Complete this survey (or, if you are a facilitator, have your CoP's members complete it) when your CoP first forms and then once per year thereafter to provide important information about your needs and experiences with the CoP.

## Demographics

1. Select the title that best describes your professional role.

- ☐ Caseworker
- ☐ Child-care provider
- ☐ Early childhood special-education teacher
- ☐ Early childhood teacher
- ☐ Early intervention provider
- ☐ Family member
- ☐ Higher-education faculty or staff
- ☐ Infant-mental-health provider
- ☐ Paraprofessional
- ☐ Part B administrator or staff
- ☐ Part C administrator or staff
- ☐ Professional-development provider
- ☐ Program manager, coordinator, or supervisor
- ☐ Service coordinator
- ☐ Student
    - ☐ Doctoral
    - ☐ Master's
    - ☐ Undergraduate
- ☐ Technical-assistance consultant or provider
- ☐ Training consultant or provider
- ☐ Other (please specify): ____________________

______________________________________________

## Participation

2. Approximately how long have you participated in your CoP's activities?

- ☐ Just started in the last month
- ☐ 2–6 months
- ☐ 7–12 months
- ☐ 1–3 years
- ☐ 4–7 years
- ☐ 8–10 years
- ☐ More than 10 years

3. How frequently have you participated in CoP activities—such as attending meetings, sharing resources with other members, and so on—in the last year (or, if the CoP has not existed that long, since the CoP began)?

- ☐ Rarely
- ☐ Sometimes
- ☐ Most of the time
- ☐ Always

4. In what ways do you participate in your CoP? Select all that apply.
   - ☐ Participate in meetings
   - ☐ Give presentations
   - ☐ Facilitate discussions or conversations
   - ☐ Post resources electronically
   - ☐ Access CoP's electronic resources
   - ☐ Share resources during discussions
   - ☐ Ask questions or request assistance from CoP members
   - ☐ Provide assistance to other CoP members
   - ☐ Participate in a subgroup formed from the original CoP
   - ☐ Am on the CoP's email list
   - ☐ Other (please specify): ______________________________

______________________________

## Value Questions

**Note:** The questions in this section are based on the report *Promoting and Assessing Value Creation in Communities and Networks* by Etienne Wenger, Beverly Trayner, and Maarten de Laat (http://www.leerarchitectuur.nl/wp-content/uploads/2013/03/Value-creation-Wenger-De-Laat-Trayner.pdf) and the "Sample—CoP Participant Evaluation" by the CoP Development Group (http://copdevelopmentgroup.pbworks.com).

### Immediate Value

5. Rate the quality of each of these types of interactions in your CoP.

| | Does Not Occur | Poor | Fair | Average | Very Good | Excellent |
|---|---|---|---|---|---|---|
| Productive discussions among members | ☐ | ☐ | ☐ | ☐ | ☐ | ☐ |
| Members getting answers to questions | ☐ | ☐ | ☐ | ☐ | ☐ | ☐ |
| Members sharing experiences | ☐ | ☐ | ☐ | ☐ | ☐ | ☐ |
| Members sharing resources or connections | ☐ | ☐ | ☐ | ☐ | ☐ | ☐ |

6. Rate the relevance of your CoP activities and interactions to your work.

- ☐ Poor
- ☐ Fair
- ☐ Average
- ☐ Very good
- ☐ Excellent

7. Rate your level of agreement with each of following statements.

| From My Participation in My CoP . . . | Strongly Disagree | Disagree | Neither Agree nor Disagree | Neither Agree nor Disagree | Strongly Agree |
|---|---|---|---|---|---|
| I have gained new knowledge and skills. | ☐ | ☐ | ☐ | ☐ | ☐ |
| I feel more confident and motivated to do my work. | ☐ | ☐ | ☐ | ☐ | ☐ |
| I have developed new relationships with colleagues. | ☐ | ☐ | ☐ | ☐ | ☐ |
| I feel supported in my role and feel that I can turn to CoP members for assistance. | ☐ | ☐ | ☐ | ☐ | ☐ |
| I have access to resources and information that I would not have easily obtained from another source. | ☐ | ☐ | ☐ | ☐ | ☐ |

 

## Applied Value

8. Which of these things have you done because of your participation in the CoP? Select all that apply.

 - ☐ I have applied information or skills that I acquired in the CoP.
 - ☐ I have used documents and resources that someone shared in the CoP.
 - ☐ I have contacted someone from the CoP as a resource or for mutual support.
 - ☐ I have collaborated with someone from the CoP on a joint project.
 - ☐ I have shared resources from the CoP with others outside the CoP.
 - ☐ I have told others about the CoP.
 - ☐ I have invited someone to join the CoP.
 - ☐ Other (please specify): ______________________________

 ______________________________

 - ☐ None of the above

 Use the following space to briefly summarize your experience with each item you selected.

 ______________________________

 ______________________________

 ______________________________

 ______________________________

 ______________________________

 

## Realized Value

9. What recognition and achievements have you acquired because of your participation in the CoP? Select all that apply.

- ☐ I have received positive feedback from a peer or supervisor on new tools I have used or shared.
- ☐ I have received positive feedback from a peer or supervisor on new skills I have demonstrated.
- ☐ I have a new network of supports that would have otherwise been difficult to establish.
- ☐ I have achieved something new in my role, such as a job opportunity, a promotion, or opportunities to lead.
- ☐ I have helped affect or contribute to programmatic changes, organizational changes, or both at a local, state, or national level.
- ☐ Other (please specify): ______________________________

______________________________

- ☐ None of the above

Use the following space to briefly summarize your experience with each item you selected.

______________________________

______________________________

______________________________

______________________________

______________________________

10. How effective has the CoP been in helping you do the following things in your role within the early childhood community?

| | N/A | Ineffective | Slightly Effective | Somewhat Effective | Moderately Effective | Very Effective |
|---|---|---|---|---|---|---|
| Support local initiatives | ☐ | ☐ | ☐ | ☐ | ☐ | ☐ |
| Support statewide initiatives | ☐ | ☐ | ☐ | ☐ | ☐ | ☐ |
| Support national initiatives | ☐ | ☐ | ☐ | ☐ | ☐ | ☐ |

## Reframing Value

11. Which of the following results have occurred because of your participation in your CoP? Select all that apply.
    - ☐ I am thinking about trying something new in my practice.
    - ☐ I am setting new goals for myself and my practice.
    - ☐ I am trying or applying something new in my practice.
    - ☐ I am changing the way that I think about or approach my work.
    - ☐ I am reframing or changing the way I have always done something.
    - ☐ Other (please specify): ____________________

      ____________________

    - ☐ None of the above

    Use the following space to briefly summarize your experience with each item you selected.

    ____________________

    ____________________

    ____________________

    ____________________

 

## Success of the CoP

12. How much effect do you think each of these factors has had on the success of the CoP?

| | Not Present | Not Sure | No Effect | Some Effect | Significant Effect |
|---|---|---|---|---|---|
| Having a shared interest with CoP members | ☐ | ☐ | ☐ | ☐ | ☐ |
| CoP members who value their participation | ☐ | ☐ | ☐ | ☐ | ☐ |
| Opportunities to network with CoP members | ☐ | ☐ | ☐ | ☐ | ☐ |
| Opportunities to network with outside professionals with different areas of expertise | ☐ | ☐ | ☐ | ☐ | ☐ |
| Strong facilitator or facilitators | ☐ | ☐ | ☐ | ☐ | ☐ |
| Effective communication that helps members stay engaged and informed | ☐ | ☐ | ☐ | ☐ | ☐ |
| Multiple ways to participate (such as in-person meetings, phone calls, web conferences, email lists, and so on) | ☐ | ☐ | ☐ | ☐ | ☐ |
| Frequencies and lengths of CoP meetings | ☐ | ☐ | ☐ | ☐ | ☐ |
| Periodic evaluation of CoP's priorities and needs | ☐ | ☐ | ☐ | ☐ | ☐ |
| Other (please specify): ______________ ______________ | ☐ | ☐ | ☐ | ☐ | ☐ |

13. How did you learn about this CoP?
    - ☐ I was a founding member.
    - ☐ A colleague invited me to come.
    - ☐ I learned about it at a conference.
    - ☐ My supervisor or administrator asked me to participate.
    - ☐ I discovered it on my own.
    - ☐ Other (please specify): ______________________________

    ______________________________________________

14. What are the greatest strengths of the CoP?

    ______________________________________________

    ______________________________________________

    ______________________________________________

    ______________________________________________

    ______________________________________________

15. What suggestions, if any, do you have to make the CoP better?

______________________________________________

______________________________________________

______________________________________________

16. What other supports do you use to help you in your role or to learn more about this CoP's shared interest? For example, do you participate in other networks or groups with people who share your interests?

______________________________________________

______________________________________________

______________________________________________

## Community Planning

17. List any discussion topics you would like to add to a future agenda.

______________________________________________

______________________________________________

______________________________________________

18. On average, how often do you visit the CoP online workspace in between meetings?

- ☐ Daily
- ☐ Weekly
- ☐ Monthly
- ☐ Never
- ☐ Other (please specify): ______________________

19. What tools would you like to see the CoP use or continue to use to help members connect between meetings? Select all that apply.

- ☐ Facebook groups
- ☐ Twitter
- ☐ Pinterest
- ☐ Google Drive (such as shared folders, Google Docs, and so on)
- ☐ Other (please specify): ______________________

 

20. Why do you visit the CoP workspace?

- ☐ To search for resources
- ☐ To see what is new after I receive an email notification
- ☐ To post a resource, comment, or question for the group
- ☐ To request resources, information, or both from the group
- ☐ Other (please specify): ____________________

  ________________________________________
- ☐ Not applicable—I never visit the CoP workspace.

21. What other comments do you wish to offer?

________________________________________

________________________________________

________________________________________

# APPENDIX F: SAMPLE ANNUAL QUALITY-RATING AND SUGGESTION SURVEY

Complete this survey (or, if you are a facilitator, have your CoP's members complete it) when your CoP first forms and then once per year thereafter to provide important information about how the CoP is working and what adjustments it might need.

## Demographics

Name: ____________________

Email address: ____________________

Phone number: ____________________

Professional role: ____________________

Organization: ____________________

City and state of residence: ____________________

How long have you worked in early childhood education? ____________________

How long have you worked in your current role? ____________________

List any special knowledge or skills that you bring to the CoP: ____________________

What interests do you want to learn more about from the CoP? ____________________

What goals (personal and/or organizational) do you hope to achieve by participating in the CoP?

____________________

When you have professional questions or concerns, what people or sources do you usually consult? ____________________

What topics would you be interested in studying in the CoP? ____________________

Would you like to take on leadership responsibilities in the CoP, such as helping plan and facilitate meetings?

☐ Yes ☐ No

List anyone (including you) whom you know who might be willing to present to the CoP as an expert guest speaker: ____________________

Circle which format(s) you prefer for CoP meetings.

In person By phone Online Other (please specify): ____________________

Circle which frequency/frequencies you prefer for CoP meetings.

Weekly Monthly Quarterly Other (please specify): ____________________

Circle which duration(s) you prefer for CoP meetings.

1 hour     90 minutes     2 hours     Half day     Full day

Other (please specify): ______________________________

Circle which time(s) of day you prefer for CoP meetings.

Mornings     Afternoons     Evenings     Specific time window (please specify): ________

Circle which day(s) of the week you prefer for CoP meetings.

Sunday     Monday     Tuesday     Wednesday     Thursday     Friday     Saturday

If you'd like to connect with other CoP members between meetings, circle which platform(s) you prefer.

Email     Blog     Online workspace     Social media (please specify): ____________

Other (please specify): ______________________________________________

Other comments or questions:

______________________________________________________________________

______________________________________________________________________

______________________________________________________________________

______________________________________________________________________

# APPENDIX G: SAMPLE PREMEETING REGISTRATION FORM AND SURVEY

Complete this survey (or, if you are a facilitator, have your CoP's members complete it) before a CoP meeting to get a sense of where the group is and what everyone wants to discuss that day. If desired, you can use this same form before every meeting.

## Demographics

1. Select the title that best describes your professional role.

- ☐ Caseworker
- ☐ Child-care provider
- ☐ Early childhood special-education teacher
- ☐ Early childhood teacher
- ☐ Early intervention provider
- ☐ Family member
- ☐ Higher-education faculty or staff
- ☐ Infant-mental-health provider
- ☐ Paraprofessional
- ☐ Part B administrator or staff
- ☐ Part C administrator or staff
- ☐ Professional-development provider
- ☐ Program manager, coordinator, or supervisor
- ☐ Service coordinator
- ☐ Student
  - ☐ Doctoral
  - ☐ Master's
  - ☐ Undergraduate
- ☐ Technical-assistance consultant or provider
- ☐ Training consultant or provider
- ☐ Other (please specify): ____________

2. Approximately how long have you worked in this role?

- ☐ Less than 6 months
- ☐ 7–12 months
- ☐ 1–3 years
- ☐ 4–7 years
- ☐ 8–10 years
- ☐ More than 10 years

3. Where do you serve children and families?

______________________________________________

______________________________________________

4. Select the response that best describes your participation in CoP meetings.

- ☐ This will be my first meeting.
- ☐ I have participated in a few meetings.
- ☐ I frequently participate in meetings.
- ☐ I never miss a meeting!
- ☐ Other (please specify): ____________ ____________

## Your Priorities

5. What updates or information would you like to share with the CoP during the next meeting?

______________________________________________

______________________________________________

______________________________________________

6. What challenge or challenges do you want to discuss during the meeting?

______________________________________________

______________________________________________

______________________________________________

7. What other comments or questions do you have?

______________________________________________

______________________________________________

______________________________________________

# APPENDIX H: SAMPLE POSTMEETING SURVEY

Complete this survey (or, if you are a facilitator, have your CoP's members complete it) directly after a CoP meeting to provide quick feedback on that meeting. If desired, you can use this same form after every meeting.

## Demographics

1. Select the title that best describes your professional role.

- ☐ Caseworker
- ☐ Child-care provider
- ☐ Early childhood special-education teacher
- ☐ Early childhood teacher
- ☐ Early intervention provider
- ☐ Family member
- ☐ Higher-education faculty or staff
- ☐ Infant-mental-health provider
- ☐ Paraprofessional
- ☐ Part B administrator or staff
- ☐ Part C administrator or staff
- ☐ Professional-development provider
- ☐ Program manager, coordinator, or supervisor
- ☐ Service coordinator
- ☐ Student
    - ☐ Doctoral
    - ☐ Master's
    - ☐ Undergraduate
- ☐ Technical-assistance consultant or provider
- ☐ Training consultant or provider
- ☐ Other (please specify): ______________________

______________________________

2. Where do you serve children and families?
Organization: ______________________________
City or town: ______________________________
State or province: ______________________________
Country: ______________________________

## Use of Time Together

3. Rate how much you valued each of the activities from this meeting.

| | Did Not Occur | Not at All | Somewhat | Greatly |
|---|---|---|---|---|
| Introductions or time to get to know one another | ☐ | ☐ | ☐ | ☐ |
| Updates | ☐ | ☐ | ☐ | ☐ |
| Show and tell | ☐ | ☐ | ☐ | ☐ |
| Sharing challenges or asking questions and getting help | ☐ | ☐ | ☐ | ☐ |
| Discussion topic or topics | ☐ | ☐ | ☐ | ☐ |
| Other (please specify): ________ ____________ | ☐ | ☐ | ☐ | ☐ |

4. What updates or information would you like to share with the CoP during the next meeting?

______________________________________________

______________________________________________

______________________________________________

## Resource Sharing and Seeking Support

5. During the meeting, did you identify at least one new strategy or idea that will help you in your role?

   ☐ Yes  ☐ No  ☐ Not sure

   If yes, please describe your experience.

______________________________________________

______________________________________________

6. Did you share any strategies or resources with others during the meeting?

   ☐ Yes  ☐ No  ☐ Not sure

   If yes, please describe your experience.

______________________________________________

______________________________________________

## Discussion Topic

7. In what ways did this meeting's discussion topic help you? Select all that apply.

    - ☐ I identified tools to support me in my role.
    - ☐ I found a new strategy I would like to try.
    - ☐ I got an idea about something I would like to develop.
    - ☐ I learned about a new person or resource that can help me in a time of need.
    - ☐ I gained confidence in my skills or abilities related to this topic.
    - ☐ Other (please specify): ______________________________

8. What other discussion topics interest you?

______________________________________________

______________________________________________

______________________________________________

9. If you would like to lead a discussion about any of your suggested topics, please provide your contact information.

    Name: ______________________________

    Email address: ______________________________

    Phone number: ______________________________

10. What other comments do you wish to offer?

______________________________________________

______________________________________________

______________________________________________

 

# REFERENCES AND RECOMMENDED READING


Barwick, Melanie, Julia Peters, and Katherine Boydell. 2009. "Getting to Uptake: Do Communities of Practice Support the Implementation of Evidence-Based Practice?" *Journal of the Canadian Academy of Child and Adolescent Psychiatry* 18(1): 16–29.

Blankenship, Selena, and Wendy Ruona. February 28–March 4, 2007. "Professional Learning Communities and Communities of Practice: A Comparison of Models, Literature Review." Paper presented at the Academy of Human Resource Development International Research Conference in the Americas, Indianapolis, IN. https://files.eric.ed.gov/fulltext/ED504776.pdf

BRIDGE. 2015. "Early Childhood Development Communities of Practice." BRIDGE. http://www.bridge.org.za/get-involved/communities-of-practice/early-childhood-development-communities-practice/

Bringle, Robert, and Julie Hatcher. 1996. "Implementing Service Learning in Higher Education." *The Journal of Higher Education* 67(2): 221–239.

Brown, John, and Paul Duguid. 1991. "Organizational Learning and Communities-of-Practice: Toward a Unified View of Working, Learning, and Innovation." *Organization Science* 2(1): 40–57.

Buysse, Virginia, Karen Sparkman, and Patricia Wesley. 2003. "Communities of Practice: Connecting What We Know with What We Do." *Exceptional Children* 69(3): 263–277.

Cashman, Joanne, Patrice Linehan, and Mariola Rosser. 2007. *Communities of Practice: A New Approach to Solving Complex Educational Problems*. Report. Alexandria, VA: National Association of State Directors of Special Education. http://www.ideapartnership.org/documents/CoPGuide.pdf

Center for IDEA Early Childhood Data Systems (DaSy). n.d. "The State Systemic Improvement Plan (SSIP)." DaSy. https://dasycenter.org/building-stakeholder-knowledge-toolkit/the-state-systemic-improvement-plan-ssip/

CenterPoint Institute. n.d. *What Is a Community of Practice? A Strategy for Achieving Desired Outcomes in the Cultures of Giving: Innovation and Impact across Communities Cluster.* Report. Mokena, IL: CenterPoint Institute. https://ccph.memberclicks.net/assets/Documents/CESToolkit/References/community%20practice%20wk%20kellogg.pdf

Centers for Disease Control and Prevention (CDC). 2019. "Communities of Practices [sic] (CoPs)." CDC. https://www.cdc.gov/phcommunities/index.html

Coffman, Karie, et al. 2016. "Waiting for the Expert to Arrive: Using a Community of Practice to Develop the Scholarly Identity of Doctoral Students." *International Journal of Teaching and Learning in Higher Education* 28(1): 30–37.

CoP Development Group. 2019. "Sample—CoP Participant Evaluation." CoP Development Group. http://copdevelopmentgroup.pbworks.com

Division for Early Childhood (DEC). 2014. *DEC Recommended Practices in Early Intervention/Early Childhood Special Education 2014*. Arlington, VA: DEC. https://divisionearlychildhood.egnyte.com/dl/tgv6GUXhVo/

Dubé, Line, Anne Bourhis, and Réal Jacob. 2006. "Towards a Typology of Virtual Communities of Practice." *Interdisciplinary Journal of Information, Knowledge, and Management* 1: 69–93. http://www.ijikm.org/Volume1/IJIKMv1p069-093Dube.pdf

Dunst, Carl. 2015. "Improving the Design and Implementation of In-Service Professional Development in Early Childhood Intervention." *Infants and Young Children* 28(3): 210–219.

Dunst, Carl, and Carol Trivette. 2009. "Using Research Evidence to Inform and Evaluate Early Childhood Intervention Practices." *Topics in Early Childhood Special Education* 29(1): 40–52.

Early Intervention–Early Childhood Professional Development Community of Practice. 2018. "Universal Online Part C EI Curriculum." Early Intervention–Early Childhood Professional Development Community of Practice. http://universalonlinepartceicurriculum.pbworks.com/w/page/79638626/Universal%20Online%20Part%20C%20EI%20Curriculum

Edgerton, Maria. 2015. *Communities of Practice: A Glimpse into Delaware*. Wheeling, IL: McCormick Center for Early Childhood Leadership at National Louis University. https://mccormick-assets.floodlight.design/wp-content/uploads/2018/03/12-28-15_CommunitiesOfPracticeAGlimpseIntoDelaware.pdf

Edmonton Regional Learning Consortium. 2016. "What Is a Community of Practice?" Edmonton Regional Learning Consortium. http://www.communityofpractice.ca/background/what-is-a-community-of-practice/

Englert, Carol Sue, and Kathi Tarrant. 1995. "Creating Collaborative Cultures for Educational Change." *Remedial and Special Education* 16(6): 325–336.

Fox, Lise, and Mary Louise Hemmeter. 2014. *Implementing Positive Behavioral Intervention and Support: The Evidence-Base of the Pyramid Model for Supporting Social Emotional Competence in Infants and Young Children*. Fort Collins, CO: Pyramid Model Consortium. https://challengingbehavior.cbcs.usf.edu/docs/Implementing-PBIS_evidence-base.pdf

Lave, Jean, and Etienne Wenger. 1991. *Situated Learning: Legitimate Peripheral Participation*. Cambridge, UK: Cambridge University Press.

Lesser, Eric, and John Storck. 2001. "Communities of Practice and Organizational Performance." *IBM Systems Journal* 40(4): 831–841.

Lipnack, Jessica, and Jeffrey Stamps. 1997. *Virtual Teams: Reaching across Space, Time, and Organizations with Technology*. New York, NY: John Wiley and Sons.

Marshall, Stephanie Pace, and Connie Hatcher. 1996. "Promoting Career Development through CADRE." *Educational Leadership* 53(6): 42–46.

McAlister, Martha. 2016. "Emerging Communities of Practice." *Collected Essays on Learning and Teaching* 9: 125–132. https://celt.uwindsor.ca/index.php/CELT/article/view/4425

McCreesh, Karen, Louise Larkin, and Jeremy Lewis. 2016. "Shouldering the Burden of Evidence-Based Practice: The Experiences of Physiotherapists Partaking in a Community of Practice." *Rehabilitation Research and Practice* 2016: 1–7. http://dx.doi.org/10.1155/2016/9051378

National Association for the Education of Young Children (NAEYC). 2009. *Developmentally Appropriate Practice in Early Childhood Programs Serving Children from Birth through Age 8*. Position statement. Washington, DC: NAEYC. https://www.naeyc.org/sites/default/files/globally-shared/downloads/PDFs/resources/position-statements/PSDAP.pdf

National Center for Educational Statistics, Institute of Education Sciences. 2017. *SLDS Issue Brief: Using ECIDS Data to Support Continuous Quality Improvement*. Issue brief. Washington, DC: National Center for Educational Statistics, Institute of Education Sciences. https://nces.grads360.org/services/PDCService.svc/GetPDCDocumentFile?fileId=28616

National Council of Teachers of English (NCTE). 2011. *Communities of Practice: A Policy Research Brief produced by the National Council of Teachers of English*. Policy research brief. Urbana, IL: James R. Squire Office of Policy Research, NCTE. https://www.ncte.org/library/NCTEFiles/Resources/Journals/CC/0212nov2011/CC0212Policy.pdf

National Implementation Research Network. n.d. "Framework 5: Improvement Cycles." National Implementation Research Network. https://nirn.fpg.unc.edu/module-1/improvement-cycles

Nichols, Sarah, et al. 2017. "The Universal Online Part C EI Curriculum—What It Is and How You Can Use It!" Zero to Three. https://email.zerotothree.org/acton/rif/18223/s-05e5-1803/-/l-2270:0/l-2270/showPreparedMessage?utm_term=Click%20here&utm_campaign=Your%20Member%20Newsletter%20from%20ZERO%20TO%20THREE&utm_content=email&utm_source=Act-On+Software&utm_medium=email&cm_mmc=Act-On%20Software-_-email-_-Your%20Member%20Newsletter%20from%20ZERO%20TO%20THREE-_-Click%20here&sid=TV2:L8MmBkd7M

Pappas, Christopher. 2014. "Top 10 Tips To Create a Corporate Learning Community of Practice." eLearning Industry. https://elearningindustry.com/top-10-tips-create-corporate-learning-community-of-practice

Piat, Myra, et al. 2016. "Recovery Communities of Practice: An Innovative Strategy for Mental Health System Transformation." *Psychiatric Services* 67(1): 10–12.

Provini, Celine. 2012. "Best Practices for Professional Learning Communities." Education World. https://www.educationworld.com/a_admin/best-practices-for-professional-learning-communities.shtml

Pyrko, Igor, Viktor Dörfler, and Colin Eden. 2016. "Thinking Together: What Makes Communities of Practice Work?" *Human Relations* 70(4): 389–409.

Ranmuthugala, Geetha, et al. 2010. *Communities of Practice in the Health Sector: A Systematic Review of the Peer-Reviewed Literature*. Sydney, Australia: Centre for Clinical Governance Research, Australian Institute of Health Innovation, Faculty of Medicine, University of New South Wales. https://pdfs.semanticscholar.org/d0ed/66832d44ae31a5dfe0cc503c9a27faed0c9e.pdf

Ranmuthugala, Geetha, et al. 2011. "How and Why Are Communities of Practice Established in the Health-Care Sector? A Systematic Review of the Literature." *BMC Health Services Research* 11(1): 273. https://bmchealthservres.biomedcentral.com/articles/10.1186/1472-6963-11-273

Rhode Island Board of Regents for Elementary and Secondary Education. 2012. *Becoming a Successful Community of Practice Facilitator*. San Francisco, CA: WestEd. http://www.ride.ri.gov/Portals/0/Uploads/Documents/Instruction-and-Assessment-World-Class-Standards/Assessment/Formative-Assessment-PD-Online-Modules/Becoming_a_Successful_CoP_Facilitator.pdf

Rogoff, Barbara. 1994. "Developing Understanding of the Idea of Communities of Learners." *Mind, Culture, and Activity* 1(4): 209–229.

Scaled Agile, Inc. 2018. "Communities of Practice." Scaled Agile, Inc. https://www.scaledagileframework.com/communities-of-practice/

Shelden, M'Lisa, and Dathan Rush. 2013. *The Early Intervention Teaming Handbook: The Primary Service Provider Approach*. Baltimore, MD: Brookes Publishing.

Social Service Institute (Singapore). 2019. "Communities of Practice." Social Service Institute (Singapore). https://www.ssi.sg/Initiatives/Communities-of-Practice

Trust, Torrey, and Brian Horrocks. 2017. "'I Never Feel Alone in My Classroom': Teacher Professional Growth within a Blended Community of Practice." *Professional Development in Education* 43(4): 645–665.

Wei, Ruth, et al. 2009. *Professional Learning in the Learning Profession: A Status Report on Teacher Development in the US and Abroad*. Technical report. Dallas, TX: National Staff Development Council. https://learningforward.org/docs/default-source/pdf/nsdcstudytechnicalreport2009.pdf

Wenger, Etienne. 1998. *Communities of Practice: Learning, Meaning, and Identity*. Cambridge, UK: Cambridge University Press.

Wenger, Etienne, Richard McDermott, and William Snyder. 2002. *Cultivating Communities of Practice: A Guide to Managing Knowledge*. Boston, MA: Harvard Business School Press.

Wenger, Etienne, and William Snyder. 2000. "Communities of Practice: The Organizational Frontier." *Harvard Business Review.* January/February. https://hbr.org/2000/01/communities-of-practice-the-organizational-frontier

Wenger, Etienne, Beverly Trayner, and Maarten de Laat. 2011. *Promoting and Assessing Value Creation in Communities and Networks: A Conceptual Framework. Report*. Heerlen, NL: Ruud de Moor Centrum. http://www.leerarchitectuur.nl/wp-content/uploads/2013/03/Value-creation-Wenger-De-Laat-Trayner.pdf

Wenger, Etienne, Nancy White, and John Smith. 2009. *Digital Habitats: Stewarding Technology for Communities*. Portland, OR: CPsquare.

Wenger-Trayner, Etienne, and Beverly Wenger-Trayner. n.d. "Levels of Participation." Wenger-Trayner.com. https://wenger-trayner.com/project/levels-of-participation/

Wenger-Trayner, Etienne, and Beverly Wenger-Trayner. 2015. "Introduction to Communities of Practice: A Brief Overview of the Concept and Its Uses." Wenger-Trayner.com. https://wenger-trayner.com/introduction-to-communities-of-practice/

Wesley, Patricia, and Virginia Buysse. 2001. "Communities of Practice: Expanding Professional Roles to Promote Reflection and Shared Inquiry." *Topics in Early Childhood Special Education* 21(2): 114–123.

Westheimer, Joel, and Joseph Kahne. 1993. "Building School Communities: An Experience-Based Model." *The Phi Delta Kappan* 75(4): 324–328.

Wheatley, Margaret, and Deborah Frieze. 2007. "Beyond Networking: How Large-Scale Change Really Happens." *School Administrator* 64(4): 35–38.

Young, Billie. 2017. *Continuous Quality Improvement in Early Childhood and School-Age Programs: An Update from the Field*. Boston, MA: BUILD Initiative and Third Sector New England. https://qrisnetwork.org/sites/all/files/session/resources/Continuous%20Quality%20Improvement%20in%20Early%20Childhood%20and%20School%20Age%20Programs%20-%20An%20Update%20from%20the%20Field.pdf

Zepeda, Sally. 2012. "How to Facilitate Job-Embedded Professional Development." Education World. https://www.educationworld.com/a_admin/job-embedded-professional-development.shtml

# INDEX

**N**



**O**



**P**

**W**



**Y**



**Z**